SECOND EDITION

Learning React Native
Building Native Mobile Apps with JavaScript

Bonnie Eisenman

Beijing · Boston · Farnham · Sebastopol · Tokyo

Learning React Native

by Bonnie Eisenman

Copyright © 2018 Bonnie Eisenman. All rights reserved.

Printed in the United States of America.

Published by O'Reilly Media, Inc., 1005 Gravenstein Highway North, Sebastopol, CA 95472.

O'Reilly books may be purchased for educational, business, or sales promotional use. Online editions are also available for most titles (*http://oreilly.com/safari*). For more information, contact our corporate/institutional sales department: 800-998-9938 or *corporate@oreilly.com*.

Editor: Meg Foley
Production Editor: Nicholas Adams
Copyeditor: Rachel Monaghan
Proofreader: Gillian McGarvey

Indexer: Judith McConville
Interior Designer: David Futato
Cover Designer: Karen Montgomery
Illustrator: Rebecca Demarest

December 2015:   First Edition
November 2017:   Second Edition

Revision History for the Second Edition
2017-10-23:   First Release

See *http://oreilly.com/catalog/errata.csp?isbn=9781491989142* for release details.

978-1-491-98914-2

[LSI]

Table of Contents

Preface

This book is an introduction to React Native, Facebook's JavaScript framework for building mobile applications. Using your existing knowledge of JavaScript and React, you'll be able to build and deploy fully featured mobile applications for both iOS and Android that truly render natively. There are plenty of advantages to working with React Native over traditional means of mobile development without needing to sacrifice the native look and feel.

We'll start with the basics and work our way up to creating a full-fledged application with 100% code reuse between iOS and Android. In addition to the essentials of the framework, we'll discuss how to work beyond it, including how to make use of third-party libraries and even how to write your own Java or Objective-C libraries to extend React Native.

If you're coming to mobile development from the perspective of a frontend software engineer or web developer, this is the book for you. React Native is a pretty amazing thing, and I hope you're as excited to explore it as I am!

Prerequisites

This book is not an introduction to React, in general. We'll assume that you have some working knowledge of React. If you're brand new to React, I suggest reading through a tutorial or two before coming back to take the plunge into mobile development. Specifically, you should be familiar with the role of props and state, the component lifecycle, and how to create React components.

We'll also be using some modern JavaScript syntax, as well as JSX. If you aren't familiar with these, don't worry; we'll cover JSX in Chapter 2, and modern JavaScript syntax in Appendix A. These features are essentially 1:1 translations of the JavaScript code you're already accustomed to writing.

This book focuses on using React Native to write iOS and Android applications, though React Native can also be used to write applications targeting Ubuntu,

Windows, and macOS. Linux and Windows users can use React Native to develop Android applications, but in order to write iOS applications, you will need to develop on macOS.

Conventions Used in This Book

The following typographical conventions are used in this book:

Italic
Indicates new terms, URLs, email addresses, filenames, and file extensions.

`Constant width`
Used for program listings, as well as within paragraphs to refer to program elements such as variable or function names, databases, data types, environment variables, statements, and keywords.

`Constant width bold`
Shows commands or other text that should be typed literally by the user.

`Constant width italic`
Shows text that should be replaced with user-supplied values or by values determined by context.

 This element signifies a tip or suggestion.

 This element signifies a general note.

 This element indicates a warning or caution.

Using Code Examples

Supplemental material (code examples, exercises, etc.) is available for download at *https://github.com/bonniee/learning-react-native*.

This book is here to help you get your job done. In general, if example code is offered with this book, you may use it in your programs and documentation. You do not need to contact us for permission unless you're reproducing a significant portion of the code. For example, writing a program that uses several chunks of code from this book does not require permission. Selling or distributing a CD-ROM of examples from O'Reilly books does require permission. Answering a question by citing this book and quoting example code does not require permission. Incorporating a significant amount of example code from this book into your product's documentation does require permission.

We appreciate, but do not require, attribution. An attribution usually includes the title, author, publisher, and ISBN. For example: "*Learning React Native, Second Edition*, by Bonnie Eisenman (O'Reilly). Copyright 2018 Bonnie Eisenman, 978-1-491-98914-2."

If you feel your use of code examples falls outside fair use or the permission given above, feel free to contact us at *permissions@oreilly.com*.

O'Reilly Safari

 *Safari* (formerly Safari Books Online) is a membership-based training and reference platform for enterprise, government, educators, and individuals.

Members have access to thousands of books, training videos, Learning Paths, interactive tutorials, and curated playlists from over 250 publishers, including O'Reilly Media, Harvard Business Review, Prentice Hall Professional, Addison-Wesley Professional, Microsoft Press, Sams, Que, Peachpit Press, Adobe, Focal Press, Cisco Press, John Wiley & Sons, Syngress, Morgan Kaufmann, IBM Redbooks, Packt, Adobe Press, FT Press, Apress, Manning, New Riders, McGraw-Hill, Jones & Bartlett, and Course Technology, among others.

For more information, please visit *http://oreilly.com/safari*.

How to Contact Us

Please address comments and questions concerning this book to the publisher:

O'Reilly Media, Inc.
1005 Gravenstein Highway North
Sebastopol, CA 95472
800-998-9938 (in the United States or Canada)
707-829-0515 (international or local)
707-829-0104 (fax)

We have a web page for this book, where we list errata, examples, and any additional information. You can access this page at *http://bit.ly/learning-react-native-2e*.

To comment or ask technical questions about this book, send email to *bookquestions@oreilly.com*.

For more information about our books, courses, conferences, and news, see our website at *http://www.oreilly.com*.

Find us on Facebook: *http://facebook.com/oreilly*

Follow us on Twitter: *http://twitter.com/oreillymedia*

Watch us on YouTube: *http://www.youtube.com/oreillymedia*

Resources

It's dangerous to go alone! Well, not really, but that doesn't mean you have to. Here are some resources you may find useful as you work through the book:

- The GitHub repository (*https://github.com/bonniee/learning-react-native*) for this book contains all of the code samples we'll be discussing. If you get stumped or want more context, try looking here first.
- Join the mailing list at LearningReactNative.com for follow-up articles, suggestions, and helpful resources.
- The official documentation (*https://facebook.github.io/react-native/*) has a lot of good reference material.

Additionally, the React Native community is a useful resource:

- The react-native tag on Stack Overflow (*http://bit.ly/react-native-so*)
- The Reactiflux (*https://www.reactiflux.com/*) chat group includes many core contributors and other helpful folks

- #reactnative (*irc.lc/freenode/reactnative*) on Freenode

Acknowledgments

As is traditional: this book would not have been possible without the help and support of many others. Thank you to my editor, Meg Foley, and the rest of the O'Reilly team for bringing this project into the world. Thank you also to my technical reviewers for your time and insightful feedback: Ryan Hurley, Dave Benjamin, David Bieber, Jason Brown, Erica Portnoy, and Jonathan Stark. I would also like to thank the React Native team, without whose stellar work this book would naturally be impossible. Thanks also to Zachary Elliott for his help with the Flashcard application, Android testing, and support throughout. Mi estas dankplena pro via subteno.

And many thanks are owed to my dear friends and family, who put up with me throughout this process and provided moral support, guidance, and distraction as the situation required. Thank you.

CHAPTER 1

What Is React Native?

React Native is a JavaScript framework for writing real, natively rendering mobile applications for iOS and Android. It's based on React, Facebook's JavaScript library for building user interfaces, but instead of targeting the browser, it targets mobile platforms. In other words, it enables web developers to write mobile applications that look and feel truly "native," all from the comfort of a familiar JavaScript library. Plus, because most of the code you write can be shared between platforms, React Native makes it easy to simultaneously develop for both Android and iOS.

Similar to React for the web, React Native applications are written with a mixture of JavaScript and XML-esque markup, known as JSX. Then, under the hood, the React Native "bridge" invokes the native rendering APIs in Objective-C (for iOS) or Java (for Android). Thus, your application will render using real mobile UI components, *not* webviews, and will look and feel like any other mobile application. React Native also exposes JavaScript interfaces for platform APIs, so your React Native apps can access platform features like the phone camera or the user's location.

The core React Native project supports writing mobile applications for both iOS and Android. Community implementations also provide support for Windows (*https:// github.com/Microsoft/react-native-windows*), Ubuntu (*https://github.com/Canoni calLtd/react-native*), the web (*https://github.com/necolas/react-native-web*), and more.

In this book, we'll build both Android and iOS apps with React Native. The vast majority of the code we write will be cross-platform.

And, yes, you can really use React Native to build production-ready mobile applications. Some anecdata: Facebook (*http://bit.ly/1YipO7A*), Airbnb (*http://bit.ly/ 2udVlOL*), Walmart (*http://bit.ly/2vuFIXk*), and Baidu (*http://bit.ly/2hzBtnr*) are already using it in production for user-facing applications.

Advantages of React Native

The fact that React Native renders using its host platform's standard rendering APIs distinguishes it from most existing methods of cross-platform application development, like Cordova or Ionic. Existing methods of writing mobile applications use combinations of JavaScript, HTML, and CSS and typically render using webviews. While this approach can work, it also comes with drawbacks, especially around performance. Additionally, these methods do not usually have access to the host platform's set of native UI elements. When these frameworks do try to mimic native UI elements, the results usually feel just a little off. In addition, reverse-engineering all the fine details of things like animations takes an enormous amount of effort, and they can quickly become outdated.

In contrast, React Native actually translates your markup to real, native UI elements, leveraging existing means of rendering views on whatever platform you are working with. Additionally, React works separately from the main UI thread, so your application can maintain high performance without sacrificing capability. The update cycle in React Native is the same as in React: when `props` or `state` change, React Native re-renders the views. The major difference between React Native and React in the browser is that React Native does this by leveraging the UI libraries of its host platform, rather than using HTML and CSS markup.

For developers accustomed to working on the web with React, this means you can write mobile apps with the performance and look and feel of a native application, while using familiar tools. React Native also represents an improvement over normal mobile development in two other areas: developer experience and cross-platform development potential.

Developer Experience

If you've developed for mobile before, you might be surprised by how easy React Native is to work with. The React Native team has baked strong developer tools and meaningful error messages into the framework so that working with robust tools is a natural part of your development experience.

For instance, because React Native is "just" JavaScript, you don't need to rebuild your application in order to see your changes reflected; instead, you can refresh your application just as you would any other web page. All of those minutes spent waiting for your application to build can really add up, and in contrast React Native's quick iteration cycle feels like a godsend.

Additionally, React Native lets you take advantage of intelligent debugging tools and error reporting. If you are comfortable with Chrome or Safari's developer tools (Figure 1-1), you will be happy to know that you can use them for mobile development as well. Likewise, you can use whatever text editor you prefer for JavaScript editing. React Native does not force you to work in Xcode to develop for iOS or in Android Studio for Android development.

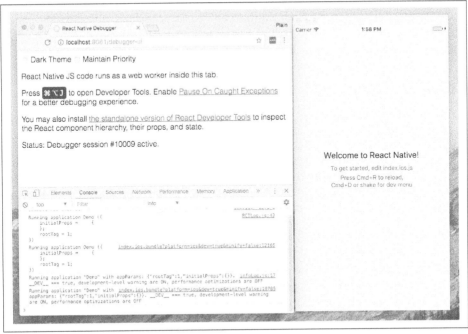

Figure 1-1. Using the Chrome Debugger with React Native

Besides the day-to-day improvements to your development experience, React Native also has the potential to positively impact your product release cycle. For instance, Apple and Google both permit you to load JavaScript-only changes to an app's behavior without going through the standard review process. This is particularly nice on iOS, where application updates typically require several days or weeks of review.

All of these small perks add up to saving you and your fellow developers time and energy, allowing you to focus on the more interesting parts of your work and be more productive overall.

Code Reuse and Knowledge Sharing

Working with React Native can dramatically shrink the resources required to build mobile applications. Any developer who knows how to write React code can target the web, iOS, and Android, all with the same skill set. By removing the need to "silo" developers based on their target platform, React Native lets your team iterate more quickly and share knowledge and resources more effectively.

Not only can you share knowledge, but much of your code can be shared, too. Not *all* the code you write will be cross-platform, and depending on the functionality you need on a specific platform, you may occasionally need to dip into Objective-C or Java (we'll cover how so-called native modules work in Chapter 7). But reusing code across platforms is surprisingly easy with React Native. For example, the Facebook Ads Manager application for Android shares 87% of its codebase with the iOS version (*https://youtu.be/PAA9O4E1IM4*). The final application we'll look at in this book, a flashcard app, has total code reuse between Android and iOS. It's hard to beat that!

Risks and Drawbacks

As with anything, using React Native is not without its downsides, and whether or not it is a good fit for your team really depends on your individual situation.

Because React Native introduces another layer to your project, it can make debugging hairier, especially at the intersection of React and the host platform. We'll cover debugging for React Native in more depth in Chapter 9 and try to address some of the most common issues.

Along the same lines, when updates are released for the host platform—say, a new suite of APIs in a new version of Android—there will be a lag before they are fully supported in React Native. The good news is that in the vast majority of cases, you can implement support for missing APIs yourself, which we'll cover in Chapter 7. Also, if you do hit a roadblock, you won't be locked in to using React Native—many companies have successfully implemented hybrid approaches to app development.

Changing the platform you use to write your applications is a big choice. Still, I think you'll see that the benefits of React Native outweigh the risks.

Summary

React Native is an exciting framework that enables web developers to create robust mobile applications using their existing JavaScript knowledge. It offers faster mobile development and more efficient code sharing across iOS, Android, and the web without sacrificing the end user's experience or application quality. The tradeoff is that it adds some complexity to your application setup. If your team can handle that and wants to develop mobile applications for more than just one platform, you should be looking at React Native.

In the next chapter, we go over some of the main ways in which React Native differs from React for the web, and cover some key concepts. If you'd like to skip straight to developing, feel free to jump to Chapter 3, in which we set up our development environment and write our very first React Native application.

CHAPTER 2

Working with React Native

In this chapter, we'll cover the *bridge*, and review how React Native works under the hood. Then, we'll look at how React Native components differ from their web counterparts, and cover what you'll need to know in order to create and style components for mobile.

 If you'd prefer to dig into the development process and see React Native in action, feel free to jump ahead to Chapter 3.

How Does React Native Work?

The idea of writing mobile applications in JavaScript feels a little odd. How is it possible to use React in a mobile environment? In order to understand the technical underpinnings of React Native, we first need to recall one of React's concepts: the Virtual DOM.

In React, the Virtual DOM acts as a layer between the developer's description of how things ought to look and the work done to actually render your application onto the page. To render interactive user interfaces in a browser, developers must edit the browser's DOM, or Document Object Model. This is an expensive step, and excessive writes to the DOM have a significant impact on performance. Rather than directly render changes on the page, React computes the necessary changes in-memory and rerenders the minimal amount necessary. Figure 2-1 shows how this works.

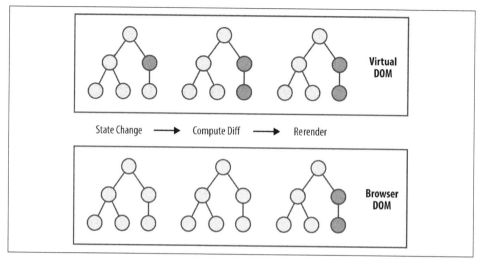

Figure 2-1. Performing calculations in the Virtual DOM limits rerendering in the browser's DOM

In the context of React on the web, most developers think of the Virtual DOM as a performance optimization. The Virtual DOM certainly has performance benefits, but its real potential lies in the power of its abstraction. Placing a clean abstraction layer between the developer's code and the actual rendering opens up a lot of interesting possibilities. What if React could render to a target other than the browser's DOM? After all, React already "understands" what your application is *supposed* to look like.

Indeed, this is how React Native works, as shown in Figure 2-2. Instead of rendering to the browser's DOM, React Native invokes Objective-C APIs to render to iOS components, or Java APIs to render to Android components. This sets React Native apart from other cross-platform app development options, which often end up rendering web-based views.

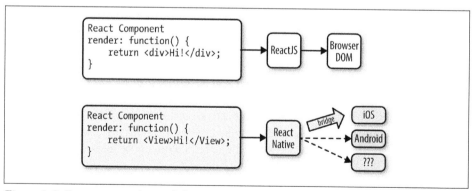

Figure 2-2. React can render to different targets

This is all possible because of the bridge, which provides React with an interface into the host platform's native UI elements. React components return markup from their render function, which describes how they should look. With React for the web, this translates directly to the browser's DOM. For React Native, this markup is translated to suit the host platform, so a <View> might become an iOS-specific UIView.

The core React Native project supports iOS and Android. Because of the abstraction layer provided by the Virtual DOM, React Native can target other platforms, too— someone just needs to write the bridge. For example, there are community implementations of React Native for Windows (*https://github.com/Microsoft/react-native-windows*) and Ubuntu (*https://github.com/CanonicalLtd/react-native*), so you can also use React Native to create desktop applications.

Rendering Lifecycle

If you are accustomed to working in React, the React lifecycle should be familiar to you. When React runs in the browser, the render lifecycle begins by mounting your React components (Figure 2-3).

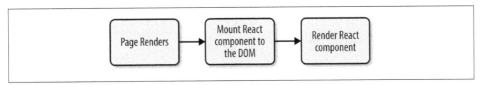

Figure 2-3. Mounting components in React

After that, React handles the rendering and rerendering of your component as necessary (Figure 2-4).

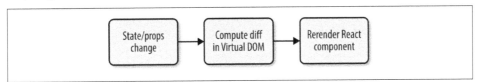

Figure 2-4. Rerendering components in React

For the render stage, the developer returns HTML markup from a React component's render method, which React then renders directly into the page as necessary.

For React Native, the lifecycle is the same, but the rendering process is slightly different because React Native depends on the bridge. We looked at the bridge briefly in Figure 2-2. The bridge translates JavaScript calls and invokes the host platform's underlying APIs and UI elements (i.e., in Objective-C or Java, as appropriate). Because React Native doesn't run on the main UI thread, it can perform these asynchronous calls without impacting the user's experience.

Creating Components in React Native

All React code lives in React components. React Native components are largely the same as ordinary React components, with some important differences around rendering and styling.

Working with Views

When writing in React for the web, you render normal HTML elements (`<div>`, `<p>`, `<span>`, `<a>`, etc.). With React Native, all of these elements are replaced by platform-specific React components (see Table 2-1). The most basic is the cross-platform `<View>`, a simple and flexible UI element that can be thought of as analogous to the `<div>`. On iOS, for instance, the `<View>` component renders to a `UIView`, whereas on Android it renders to a `View`.

Table 2-1. Basic React elements for the web compared with React Native

React	React Native
`<div>`	`<View>`
`<span>`	`<Text>`
`<li>, <ul>`	`<FlastList>`, child items
`<img>`	`<Image>`

Other components are platform-specific. For instance, the `<DatePickerIOS>` component (predictably) renders the iOS standard date picker (Figure 2-5). Here is an excerpt from the `RNTester` sample app, demonstrating an iOS date picker. The usage is straightforward, as you would expect:

```
<DatePickerIOS
  date={this.state.date}
  mode="time"
/>
```

Figure 2-5. The <DatePickerIOS> component is, as the name suggests, iOS-specific

---

Because all of our UI elements are now React components rather than basic HTML elements like the `<div>`, you will need to explicitly import each component you want to use. For instance, we need to import the `<DatePickerIOS>` component like so:

```
import { DatePickerIOS } from "react-native";
```

The `RNTester` application, which is bundled into the React Native GitHub project (*https://github.com/facebook/react-native/tree/master/RNTester*), allows you to view all of the supported UI elements. I encourage you to examine the various elements included in the `RNTester` app. It also demonstrates many styling options and interactions.

 Platform-specific components and APIs have special tags in the documentation, and typically use the platform name as a suffix —for example, `<TabBarIOS>` and `<ToolbarAndroid>`.

Because these components vary from platform to platform, how you structure your React components becomes even more important when you're working in React Native. In React for the web, we often have a mix of React components: some manage logic and their child components, while others render raw markup. If you want to reuse code when working in React Native, maintaining separation between these types of components becomes critical. A React `<DatePickerIOS>` component obviously cannot be reused for Android. However, a component that encapsulates the associated *logic* can be reused. Then the visual component can be swapped out based on your platform. You can also designate platform-specific versions of components if you want, so you could have a *picker.ios.js* and a *picker.android.js* file, each with a separate implementation of the same component. We'll cover this in "Components with Platform-Specific Implementations" on page 134.

Using JSX

In React Native, just as in React, we write our views using JSX, combining markup and the JavaScript that controls it into a single file. JSX met with strong reactions when React first debuted. For many web developers, the separation of files based on technologies is a given: you keep your CSS, HTML, and JavaScript files separate. The idea of combining markup, control logic, and even styling into one language can be confusing.

JSX prioritizes the separation of *concerns* over the separation of technologies. In React Native, this is even more strictly enforced. In a world without the browser, it makes even more sense to unify our styles, markup, and behavior in a single file for each component. Accordingly, your *.js* files in React Native are in fact JSX files. If you've been using vanilla JavaScript when working with React for the web, you will want to transition to JSX syntax for your work in React Native.

If you've never seen JSX before, don't worry: it's pretty simple. As an example, a pure-JavaScript React component for the web might look something like this:

```
class HelloMessage extends React.Component {
  render() {
    return React.createElement(
      "div",
      null,
      "Hello ",
      this.props.name
    );
  }
}

ReactDOM.render(
  React.createElement(HelloMessage, { name: "Bonnie" }), mountNode);
```

We can render this more succinctly by using JSX. Instead of calling `React.createElement` and passing in a list of HTML attributes, we use XML-like markup:

```
class HelloMessage extends Component {
  render() {
    // Instead of calling createElement, we return markup
    return <div>Hello {this.props.name}</div>;
  }
}

// We no longer need a createElement call here
ReactDOM.render(<HelloMessage name="Bonnie" />, mountNode);
```

Both of these will render the following HTML onto the page:

```
<div>Hello Bonnie</div>
```

Styling Native Components

On the web, we style React components using CSS, just as we would any other HTML element. Whether you love it or hate it, CSS is a necessary part of the web. React usually does not affect the way we write CSS. It does make it easier to dynamically build class names based on props and state, but otherwise React is mostly agnostic about how we handle styles on the web.

Non-web platforms have a wide array of approaches to layout and styling. When we work with React Native, thankfully, we utilize one standardized approach to styling. Part of the bridge between React and the host platform includes the implementation of a heavily pruned subset of CSS. This narrow implementation of CSS relies primarily on flexbox for layout, and focuses on simplicity rather than implementing the full range of CSS rules. Unlike the web, where CSS support varies across browsers, React Native is able to enforce consistent support of style rules. As with the various UI elements, you can see many examples of supported styles in the RNTester (*https://github.com/facebook/react-native/tree/master/RNTester*) application, which is one of the examples that ships with React Native.

React Native also insists on the use of inline styles, which exist as JavaScript objects. The React team has advocated for this approach before in React for web applications. If you have previously experimented with inline styles in React, the syntax will look familiar to you:

```
// Define a style...
const style = {
  backgroundColor: 'white',
  fontSize: '16px'
};

// ...and then apply it.
const txt = (
  <Text style={style}>
    A styled Text
  </Text>);
```

React Native also provides some utilities for creating and extending style objects that make dealing with inline styles a more manageable process. We will explore those later in Chapter 5.

Does looking at inline styles make you twitch? If you're coming from a web-based background, this is a break from standard practices. Working with style objects, as opposed to stylesheets, takes some mental adjustments and changes the way you need to approach writing styles. However, in the context of React Native, it is a useful shift. We will be discussing styling best practices and workflow in Chapter 5. Just try not to be surprised when you see them in use!

Host Platform APIs

Perhaps the biggest difference between React for the web and React Native is the way we think about host platform APIs. On the web, we often deal with fragmentation and inconsistent adoption of standards; still, most browsers support a common core of shared features. With React Native, however, platform-specific APIs play a much larger role in creating an excellent, natural-feeling user experience. There are also many more options to consider. Mobile APIs include everything from data storage to location services to accessing hardware such as the camera. Unconventional platforms lead to even more interesting APIs—what should the interface look like between React Native and a virtual reality headset, for instance?

By default, React Native for iOS and Android includes support for many commonly used features, and React Native can support any asynchronous native API. We will take a look at many of them throughout this book. React Native makes it straightforward and simple to use host platform APIs, so you can experiment freely. Be sure to think about what feels *right* for your target platform, and design with natural interactions in mind.

Inevitably, the React Native bridge will not expose all host platform functionality. If you find yourself in need of an unsupported feature, you have the option of adding it to React Native yourself. Alternatively, chances are good that someone else has done so already, so be sure to check for community implementations. We'll cover this in Chapter 7.

It is also worth noting that utilizing host platform APIs has implications for code reuse. React components that need platform-specific functionality will be platform-specific as well. Isolating and encapsulating those components will bring added flexibility to your application. Of course, this applies for the web, too: if you plan on sharing code between React Native and React, keep in mind that things like the DOM do not actually exist in React Native.

Summary

Writing components for mobile is a bit different in React Native when compared with React for the web. JSX is mandatory, and our basic building blocks are now components such as <View> in lieu of HTML elements such as <div>. Styling is also quite different, based on a subset of CSS, and we assign styles with inline syntax. Still, these adjustments are quite manageable. In the next chapter, we'll put this into practice as we build our first application!

CHAPTER 3

Building Your First Application

In this chapter, we will cover how to set up your local development environment for working with React Native. Then we will go through the basics of creating a simple application that you can deploy to your own iOS or Android device.

Setting Up Your Environment

Setting up your development environment will enable you to follow along with the examples in the book and write your own applications.

There are two general approaches to setting up a development environment for React Native. The first, a tool called Create React Native App, gives you a quicker, easier installation but supports only pure-JavaScript applications. The second, more traditional approach involves fully installing React Native and all of its dependencies. Think of Create React Native App as a shortcut for easier testing and prototyping.

Information on migrating from Create React Native App to a full React Native project can be found in Appendix C.

Which approach should you take? I recommend that beginners use Create React Native App for educational purposes and quick prototyping.

Eventually, if you're working on a React Native app professionally or writing a hybrid app that uses both JavaScript and native Java, Objective-C, or Swift code, you'll want to install the full React Native developer setup.

Both approaches are described next. The example code in subsequent chapters will typically work with either approach; when something is incompatible with Create React Native App and requires a full React Native project, it will be noted.

Developer Setup: Create React Native App

Create React Native App (*https://github.com/react-community/create-react-native-app*) is a command-line tool that allows you to quickly create and run React Native applications without needing to install Xcode or Android Studio.

If you want to get up and running quickly, then Create React Native App is the right choice.

 Create React Native App is a great tool, but as mentioned earlier it supports only pure-JavaScript applications. Later in this book, we'll discuss ways of integrating React Native applications with native code written in Java or Objective-C. Don't worry: if you begin with Create React Native App, you can still "eject" into a full React Native project.

Let's start by installing the create-react-native-app package from npm. React Native uses npm, the Node.js package manager, to manage dependencies. The npm registry includes packages for all sorts of JavaScript projects, not just Node.

```
npm install -g create-react-native-app
```

Creating Your First Application with create-react-native-app

To create a new project with Create React Native App, run the following command:

```
create-react-native-app first-project
```

This will install some JavaScript dependencies, as well as create the boilerplate for your application. Your project directory will look something like this:

```
.
├── App.js
├── App.test.js
├── README.md
├── app.json
├── node_modules
├── package.json
└── yarn.lock
```

This structure looks like what you might expect from a simple JavaScript project. There is a *package.json* file, which contains metadata about the project and its dependencies. The *README.md* file includes information for running the project. *App.test.js* includes a simple test file. The code for your application is located in

---

App.js. To modify this project and build out your own application, you would begin with *App.js*.

We will cover what this code is doing in more detail once we start building our weather application in "Building a Weather App" on page 22.

Previewing Your App on iOS or Android

Great—now your application is ready for testing. To launch your application, run:

```
cd first-project
npm start
```

You should see the screen shown in Figure 3-1.

Figure 3-1. Previewing a Create React Native App by using a QR code

In order to view your application, you'll need the Expo app (*https://expo.io/*) for iOS or Android. Once you have it installed, point your phone's camera at the QR code, and your React Native app will load. Note that your phone and computer will need to be on the same network, and able to communicate with each other.

Congrats! You've created your first React Native app, compiled it, and gotten it running on a real device.

In the next section, we'll cover how to do a full, traditional installation of React Native. You can skip to "Exploring the Sample Code" on page 19 instead if you'd like to get started programming.

Developer Setup: The Traditional Approach

Instructions for installing React Native and all of its dependencies can be found in the official React Native documentation (*http://facebook.github.io/react-native/*).

You can use Windows, macOS, or Linux to develop applications with React Native. However, macOS is required to develop iOS applications. Linux and Windows users can still use React Native to write Android applications.

Because the setup instructions vary by platform and React Native version, we won't go into them in detail here, but you'll need to set up the following:

- node.js
- React Native
- iOS development environment (Xcode)
- Android development environment (JDK, Android SDK, Android Studio)

If you don't want to install developer tools for both iOS and Android, that's fine—just make sure that you have at least one of them set up.

Creating Your First Application with react-native

You can use the React Native command-line tools to create a new application. Run the following command to install the command-line tools:

```
npm install -g react-native-cli
```

Now we can generate a fresh project with all of the React Native, iOS, and Android boilerplate we'll need by running:

```
react-native init FirstProject
```

The resulting directory structure should look similar to the following:

```
.
├── __tests__
├── android
├── app.json
├── index.android.js
├── index.ios.js
├── ios
├── node_modules
├── package.json
└── yarn.lock
```

The *ios/* and *android/* directories contain boilerplate relevant to those platforms. Your React code is located in the *index.ios.js* and *android.ios.js* files, which are the respective entry points for your React application. Dependencies installed via npm can, as usual, be found in the *node_modules/* folder.

Running Your App on iOS

To run your app on iOS, start by navigating into your newly created project's directory. Then you can run your React Native application like so:

```
cd FirstProject
react-native run-ios
```

Alternatively, you can open your application in Xcode and launch the iOS simulator from there:

```
open ios/FirstProject.xcodeproj
```

You can also use Xcode to upload your application to a real device for testing. In order to do this, you will need a free Apple ID so that you can configure code signing.

To configure code signing, open your project in the Xcode Project Navigator and select your main target, which should have the same name as your project. Next, select the General tab. Under the Signing menu, select your Apple developer account from the Team drop-down (see Figure 3-2). You will then need to repeat this step for the Tests target.

Figure 3-2. Setting the Team in Xcode will allow you to test your application on a physical device

The first time you attempt to run your application on any particular device, Xcode will prompt you to sign into your Apple account and register your device for development.

For more details on how to run your app on a real iOS device, check out Apple's official documentation (*http://apple.co/2gcjVhy*).

Note that your iOS device and your computer must be on the same network in order for your application to run.

Running Your App on Android

In order to run your application on Android, you need a fully functioning Android developer setup, including Android Studio and the Android SDK. See the Getting Started (*https://facebook.github.io/react-native/docs/getting-started.html*) documentation for a list of Android dependencies.

To launch your React Native platform on Android, run:

```
react-native run-android
```

You can also open your application in Android Studio and compile and run it from there.

You can either run your application in the Android emulator or on a physical device connected via USB. In order to run on a physical device, you will need to enable USB debugging in your device's Developer Options. More detailed instructions are available in the Android Studio documentation (*https://developer.android.com/studio/debug/dev-options.html*).

Exploring the Sample Code

Now that you have launched and deployed the default application, let's figure out how it works. In this section, we will dig into the source code of the default application and explore the structure of a React Native project.

If you are using Create React Native App, open the file *App.js* (see Example 3-1). If you are using a full React Native project, open up *index.ios.js* or *index.android.js* (see Example 3-2).

Example 3-1. The starter code in App.js, for Create React Native App projects

```
import React from "react";
import { StyleSheet, Text, View } from "react-native";

export default class App extends React.Component {
  render() {
    return (
      <View style={styles.container}>
        <Text>Hello, world!</Text>
      </View>
    );
  }
}

const styles = StyleSheet.create({
  container: {
    flex: 1,
    backgroundColor: "#fff",
    alignItems: "center",
    justifyContent: "center"
  }
});
```

Example 3-2. The starter code in index.ios.js and index.android.js, for full React Native projects

```
import React, { Component } from 'react';
import {
  AppRegistry,
  StyleSheet,
  Text,
  View
} from 'react-native';

export default class FirstProject extends Component {
  render() {
    return (
      <View style={styles.container}>
```

```
        <Text style={styles.welcome}>
          Welcome to React Native!
        </Text>
        <Text style={styles.instructions}>
          To get started, edit index.ios.js
        </Text>
        <Text style={styles.instructions}>
          Press Cmd+R to reload,{'\n'}
          Cmd+D or shake for dev menu
        </Text>
      </View>
    );
  }
}

const styles = StyleSheet.create({
  container: {
    flex: 1,
    justifyContent: 'center',
    alignItems: 'center',
    backgroundColor: '#F5FCFF',
  },
  welcome: {
    fontSize: 20,
    textAlign: 'center',
    margin: 10,
  },
  instructions: {
    textAlign: 'center',
    color: '#333333',
    marginBottom: 5,
  },
});

AppRegistry.registerComponent('FirstProject', () => FirstProject);
```

Either way, let's talk about what's going on here.

As you can see in Example 3-3, the import statements used are a bit different than what you might expect from a web-based React project.

Example 3-3. Importing UI elements in React Native

```
import React, { Component } from "react";
import {
  StyleSheet,
  Text,
  View
} from "react-native";
```

There's some interesting syntax going on here. React is imported as usual, but what is happening on the next line?

One quirk of working with React Native is that you need to explicitly import every Native-provided module you work with. Elements like <div> don't simply exist; instead, you need to explicitly import components such as <View> and <Text>. Library functions such as Stylesheet and AppRegistry also must be explicitly imported with this syntax. Once we start building our own applications, we will explore the other React Native functions that you may need to import.

If the syntax is unfamiliar to you, check out Example A-4 in Appendix A for an explanation of destructuring in ES6.

Next, let's look at the component class in Example 3-4. This should all look comfortably familiar because it's an ordinary React component. The main difference is its use of <Text> and <View> components instead of <div> and <span>, and the use of style objects.

Example 3-4. FirstProject component, with styles

```
export default class FirstProject extends Component {
  render() {
    return (
      <View style={styles.container}>
        <Text style={styles.welcome}>
          Welcome to React Native!
        </Text>
        <Text style={styles.instructions}>
          To get started, edit index.ios.js
        </Text>
        <Text style={styles.instructions}>
          Press Cmd+R to reload,{'\n'}
          Cmd+D or shake for dev menu
        </Text>
      </View>
    );
  }
}

const styles = StyleSheet.create({
  container: {
    flex: 1,
    justifyContent: 'center',
    alignItems: 'center',
    backgroundColor: '#F5FCFF',
  },
  welcome: {
    fontSize: 20,
    textAlign: 'center',
```

```
    margin: 10,
  },
  instructions: {
    textAlign: 'center',
    color: '#333333',
    marginBottom: 5,
  },
});
```

As I mentioned earlier, all styling in React Native is done with style objects rather than stylesheets. The standard method of handling styling is by utilizing the Style Sheet library. You can see how the style objects are defined toward the bottom of the file. Note that only <Text> components can take text-specific styles like fontSize, and that all layout logic is handled by flexbox. We will discuss how to build layouts with flexbox at greater length in Chapter 5.

The sample application is a good demonstration of the basic functions you will need to create React Native applications. It mounts a React component for rendering and demonstrates the basics of styling and rendering in React Native. It also gives us a simple way to test our development setup and try deploying to a real device. However, it's still a very basic application with no user interaction. So now let's try building a more full-featured application.

Building a Weather App

In this section, we will be building off of the sample application to create a weather app. This will give us a chance to explore how to utilize and combine stylesheets, flexbox, network communication, user input, and images into a useful app we can then deploy to an Android or iOS device.

This section may feel like a bit of a blur, as it will be giving you an overview of these features rather than deep explanations of them. The weather app will serve as a useful reference in future sections as we discuss these features in more detail, however, so don't worry if it feels like we're moving quickly!

As shown in Figure 3-3, the final application includes a text field where users can input a zip code. It will then fetch data from the OpenWeatherMap API and display the current weather.

Figure 3-3. The finished weather app

The first thing we'll do is replace the default code from our sample app. Move the initial component out into its own file, *WeatherProject.js*.

If you created a full React Native project, you will need to replace the contents of *index.ios.js* and *index.android.js*, as shown in Example 3-5.

Example 3-5. Simplified contents of index.ios.js and index.android.js (they should be identical)

```
import { AppRegistry } from "react-native";
import WeatherProject from "./WeatherProject";
AppRegistry.registerComponent("WeatherProject", () => WeatherProject);
```

Similarly, if you created a React Native project with Create React Native App, you will need to replace the contents of *App.js*, as shown in Example 3-6.

Example 3-6. Simplified contents of App.js for Create React Native App projects

```
import WeatherProject from "./WeatherProject";
export default WeatherProject;
```

Handling User Input

We want the user to be able to enter a zip code and get the forecast for that area, so we need to add a text field for user input. We can start by adding zip code information to our component's initial state (see Example 3-7).

Example 3-7. Adding zip code information to your component, before the render function

```
constructor(props) {
  super(props);
  this.state = { zip: "" };
}
```

If you're accustomed to using `React.createClass()` to create components instead of JavaScript classes, this may seem odd. When creating component classes, we set the initial `state` values for React components by mutating the `this.state` variable in the `constructor` method. If you need a review of the React component lifecycle, see the React docs (*https://facebook.github.io/react/docs/react-component.html*).

Next, we should also change one of the `<Text>` components to display `this.state.zip`, as shown in Example 3-8.

Example 3-8. Adding a <Text> component that displays the current zip code

```
<Text style={styles.welcome}>
  You input {this.state.zip}.
</Text>
```

With that out of the way, let's add a `<TextInput>` component (see Example 3-9). This is a basic component that allows the user to enter text.

Example 3-9. The <TextInput> component is used for entering text

```
<TextInput
  style={styles.input}
  onSubmitEditing={this._handleTextChange}/>
```

The `<TextInput>` component is documented in the React Native docs (*http://facebook.github.io/react-native/docs/textinput.html#content*), along with its properties. You can also pass the `<TextInput>` additional callbacks in order to listen to other events, such as `onChange` or `onFocus`, but we do not need them at the moment.

Note that we've added a simple style to the `<TextInput>`. Add the `input` style to your stylesheet like so:

```
const styles = StyleSheet.create({
  ...
  input: {
    fontSize: 20,
    borderWidth: 2,
    height: 40
    }
  ...
});
```

The callback we passed as the onSubmitEditing prop should be added as a function on the component, as shown in Example 3-10.

Example 3-10. The handleText callback for our <TextInput>

```
_handleTextChange = event => {
 this.setState({zip: event.nativeEvent.text})
}
```

By using fat-arrow syntax, we ensure that our callback is properly bound to the component instance. React autobinds lifecycle methods such as render, but for other methods we need to pay attention to binding. Fat-arrow functions are covered in Example A-8.

You will also need to update your import statements, as shown in Example 3-11.

Example 3-11. Importing UI elements in React Native

```
import {
  ...
  TextInput
  ...
} from "react-native;
```

Now try running your application using either the iOS simulator or the Android emulator. It won't be pretty, but you should be able to successfully submit a zip code and see it reflected in the <Text> component.

If we wanted, we could add some simple input validation here to ensure that the user typed in a five-digit number, but we will skip that for now.

Example 3-12 shows the full code for the *WeatherProject.js* component thus far.

Example 3-12. This version of WeatherProject.js simply accepts and records user input

```
import React, { Component } from "react";

import { StyleSheet, Text, View, TextInput } from "react-native";
```

```
class WeatherProject extends Component {
  constructor(props) {
    super(props);
    this.state = { zip: "" };
  }

  _handleTextChange = event => {
    this.setState({ zip: event.nativeEvent.text });
  };

  render() {
    return (
      <View style={styles.container}>
        <Text style={styles.welcome}>
          You input {this.state.zip}.
        </Text>
        <TextInput
          style={styles.input}
          onSubmitEditing={this._handleTextChange}
        />
      </View>
    );
  }
}

const styles = StyleSheet.create({
  container: {
    flex: 1,
    justifyContent: "center",
    alignItems: "center",
    backgroundColor: "#F5FCFF"
  },
  welcome: { fontSize: 20, textAlign: "center", margin: 10 },
  input: {
    fontSize: 20,
    borderWidth: 2,
    padding: 2,
    height: 40,
    width: 100,
    textAlign: "center"
  }
});

export default WeatherProject;
```

Displaying Data

Now let's work on displaying the forecast for that zip code. We will start by adding some mock data to our initial state value in *WeatherProject.js*:

```
constructor(props) {
  super(props);
```

```
    this.state = { zip: "", forecast: null };
  }
```

For sanity's sake, let's also pull the forecast rendering into its own component. Make a new file called *Forecast.js* (see Example 3-13).

Example 3-13. <Forecast> component in Forecast.js

```
import React, { Component } from "react";

import { StyleSheet, Text, View } from "react-native";

class Forecast extends Component {
  render() {
    return (
      <View style={styles.container}>
        <Text style={styles.bigText}>
          {this.props.main}
        </Text>
        <Text style={styles.mainText}>
          Current conditions: {this.props.description}
        </Text>
        <Text style={styles.bigText}>
          {this.props.temp}°F
        </Text>
      </View>
    );
  }
}

const styles = StyleSheet.create({
  container: { height: 130 },
  bigText: {
    flex: 2,
    fontSize: 20,
    textAlign: "center",
    margin: 10,
    color: "#FFFFFF"
  },
  mainText: { flex: 1, fontSize: 16, textAlign: "center", color: "#FFFFFF" }
});

export default Forecast;
```

The <Forecast> component just renders some <Text> based on its props. We've also included some simple styles at the bottom of the file to control things like text color.

Import the <Forecast> component and then add it to your app's render method, passing it props based on this.state.forecast (see Example 3-14). We'll address issues with layout and styling later. You can see how the <Forecast> component appears in the resulting application in Figure 3-4.

Example 3-14. WeatherProject.js, updated to include the <Forecast> component

```
import React, { Component } from "react";

import { StyleSheet, Text, View, TextInput } from "react-native";
import Forecast from "./Forecast";

class WeatherProject extends Component {
  constructor(props) {
    super(props);
    this.state = { zip: "", forecast: null };
  }

  _handleTextChange = event => {
    this.setState({ zip: event.nativeEvent.text });
  };

  render() {
    let content = null;
    if (this.state.forecast !== null) {
      content = (
        <Forecast
          main={this.state.forecast.main}
          description={this.state.forecast.description}
          temp={this.state.forecast.temp}
        />
      );
    }

    return (
      <View style={styles.container}>
        <Text style={styles.welcome}>
          You input {this.state.zip}.
        </Text>
        {content}
        <TextInput
          style={styles.input}
          onSubmitEditing={this._handleTextChange}
        />
      </View>
    );
  }
}

const styles = StyleSheet.create({
  container: {
    flex: 1,
    justifyContent: "center",
```

```
    alignItems: "center",
    backgroundColor: "#F5FCFF"
  },
  welcome: { fontSize: 20, textAlign: "center", margin: 10 },
  input: {
    fontSize: 20,
    borderWidth: 2,
    padding: 2,
    height: 40,
    width: 100,
    textAlign: "center"
  }
});

export default WeatherProject;
```

Because we still don't have a forecast to render, nothing should change visually yet.

Fetching Data from the Web

Next, let's explore using the networking APIs available in React Native. You won't be using jQuery to send AJAX requests from mobile devices. Instead, React Native implements the Fetch API. The Promise-based syntax, shown in Example 3-15, is fairly simple.

Example 3-15. Using the React Native Fetch API

```
fetch('http://www.somesite.com')
  .then((response) => response.text())
  .then((responseText) => {
    console.log(responseText);
  });
```

If you're not accustomed to working with Promises, see "Working with Promises" on page 213.

We will be using the OpenWeatherMap API, which provides us with a simple endpoint that returns the current weather for a given zip code. A small library for this API is provided in *open_weather_map.js*, shown in Example 3-16.

Example 3-16. The OpenWeatherMap library, from src/weather/open_weather_map.js

```
const WEATHER_API_KEY = "bbeb34ebf60ad50f7893e7440a1e2b0b";
const API_STEM = "http://api.openweathermap.org/data/2.5/weather?";

function zipUrl(zip) {
  return `${API_STEM}q=${zip}&units=imperial&APPID=${WEATHER_API_KEY}`;
}
```

```
function fetchForecast(zip) {
  return fetch(zipUrl(zip))
    .then(response => response.json())
    .then(responseJSON => {
      return {
        main: responseJSON.weather[0].main,
        description: responseJSON.weather[0].description,
        temp: responseJSON.main.temp
      };
    })
    .catch(error => {
      console.error(error);
    });
}

export default { fetchForecast: fetchForecast };
```

Let's import it now:

```
import OpenWeatherMap from "./open_weather_map";
```

To integrate it into our application, we can change the callback on the <TextInput>
component to query the OpenWeatherMap API, as shown in Example 3-17.

Example 3-17. Fetching data from the OpenWeatherMap API

```
_handleTextChange = event => {
  let zip = event.nativeEvent.text;
  OpenWeatherMap.fetchForecast(zip).then(forecast => {
    console.log(forecast);
    this.setState({ forecast: forecast });
  });
};
```

Logging the forecast here is a nice sanity check for us; for more detailed information
on how to view the console output, see "Debugging with console.log" on page 141.

Finally, we also need to update the styling for our container so that we can see the
forecast text render:

```
    container: {
      flex: 1,
      justifyContent: "center",
      alignItems: "center",
      backgroundColor: "#666666"
    }
```

Now, when you enter a zip code, you should actually see a forecast render
(Figure 3-4).

Figure 3-4. The weather app so far

The updated code for *WeatherProject.js* is shown in Example 3-18.

Example 3-18. WeatherProject.js: now with real data!

```
import React, { Component } from "react";

import { StyleSheet, Text, View, TextInput } from "react-native";
import OpenWeatherMap from "./open_weather_map";
import Forecast from "./Forecast";

class WeatherProject extends Component {
  constructor(props) {
    super(props);
    this.state = { zip: "", forecast: null };
  }

  _handleTextChange = event => {
    let zip = event.nativeEvent.text;
    OpenWeatherMap.fetchForecast(zip).then(forecast => {
      this.setState({ forecast: forecast });
    });
  };
```

```
render() {
  let content = null;
  if (this.state.forecast !== null) {
    content = (
      <Forecast
        main={this.state.forecast.main}
        description={this.state.forecast.description}
        temp={this.state.forecast.temp}
      />
    );
  }

  return (
    <View style={styles.container}>
      <Text style={styles.welcome}>
        You input {this.state.zip}.
      </Text>
      {content}
      <TextInput
        style={styles.input}
        onSubmitEditing={this._handleTextChange}
      />
    </View>
  );
}
}

const styles = StyleSheet.create({
  container: {
    flex: 1,
    justifyContent: "center",
    alignItems: "center",
    backgroundColor: "#666666"
  },
  welcome: { fontSize: 20, textAlign: "center", margin: 10 },
  input: {
    fontSize: 20,
    borderWidth: 2,
    padding: 2,
    height: 40,
    width: 100,
    textAlign: "center"
  }
});

export default WeatherProject;
```

Adding a Background Image

Plain background colors are boring. Let's display a background image to go along with our forecast.

Image assets are managed much like any other code asset: you can include them with a `require` call. We are going to use a file called *flowers.png* as our background image. It can be required like so:

```
<Image source={require('./flowers.png')}/>
```

The image file is available in the GitHub repository (*https://github.com/bonniee/learning-react-native/blob/2.0.0/src/weather/flowers.png*).

Just like JavaScript assets, if you have a *flowers.ios.png* and a *flowers.android.png* file, the React Native packager will load the appropriate image based on the platform. Likewise, you can use the @2x and @3x suffixes to provide different image files for different screen densities. So, hypothetically, we could structure our project directory like so:

```
.
├── flowers.png
├── flowers@2x.png
├── flowers@3x.png
...
```

To add a background image to a `<View>`, we don't set a `background` property on a `<div>` like we do on the web. Instead, we use an `<Image>` component as a container:

```
<Image source={require('./flowers.png')}
       resizeMode='cover'
       style={styles.backdrop}>
  // Your content here
</Image>
```

The `<Image>` component expects a `source` prop, which we get by using `require`.

Don't forget to style it with `flexDirection` so that its children render as we'd like them to:

```
backdrop: {
  flex: 1,
  flexDirection: 'column'
}
```

Now let's give the `<Image>` some children. Update the `render` method of the `<Weather Project>` component to return the following:

```
<View style={styles.container}>
  <Image
    source={require("./flowers.png")}
    resizeMode="cover"
    style={styles.backdrop}>
    <View style={styles.overlay}>
      <View style={styles.row}>
        <Text style={styles.mainText}>
          Current weather for
```

```
    </Text>
    <View style={styles.zipContainer}>
      <TextInput
        style={[styles.zipCode, styles.mainText]}
        onSubmitEditing={event => this._handleTextChange(event)}
      />
    </View>
  </View>
  {content}
  </View>
  </Image>
</View>
```

You'll notice that I'm using some additional styles that we haven't discussed yet, such as row, overlay, zipContainer, and zipCode. You can skip ahead to Example 3-19 to see the full stylesheet.

Putting It All Together

For the final version of the application, I've reorganized the <WeatherProject> component's render function and tweaked the styles. The main change is to the layout logic, which is diagrammed in Figure 3-5.

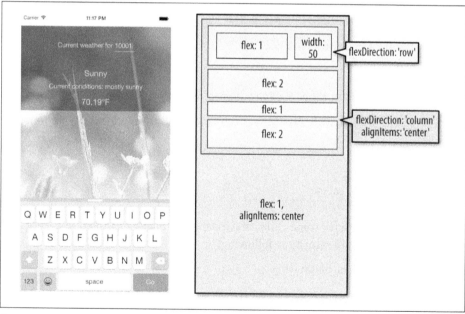

Figure 3-5. Layout of the finished weather application

Okay, ready to see it all in one place? Example 3-19 shows the finished code for the <WeatherProject> component in full, including the stylesheets. The <Forecast> component will be the same as shown previously in Example 3-13.

Example 3-19. Finished code for WeatherProject.js

```
import React, { Component } from "react";

import { StyleSheet, Text, View, TextInput, Image } from "react-native";

import Forecast from "./Forecast";
import OpenWeatherMap from "./open_weather_map";

class WeatherProject extends Component {
  constructor(props) {
    super(props);
    this.state = { zip: "", forecast: null };
  }

  _handleTextChange = event => {
    let zip = event.nativeEvent.text;
    OpenWeatherMap.fetchForecast(zip).then(forecast => {
      this.setState({ forecast: forecast });
    });
  };

  render() {
    let content = null;
    if (this.state.forecast !== null) {
      content = (
        <Forecast
          main={this.state.forecast.main}
          description={this.state.forecast.description}
          temp={this.state.forecast.temp}
        />
      );
    }
    return (
      <View style={styles.container}>
        <Image
          source={require("./flowers.png")}
          resizeMode="cover"
          style={styles.backdrop}
        >
          <View style={styles.overlay}>
            <View style={styles.row}>
              <Text style={styles.mainText}>
                Current weather for
              </Text>
              <View style={styles.zipContainer}>
                <TextInput
```

```
                    style={[styles.zipCode, styles.mainText]}
                    onSubmitEditing={this._handleTextChange}
                    underlineColorAndroid="transparent"
                />
              </View>
            </View>
            {content}
          </View>
        </Image>
      </View>
    );
  }
}

const baseFontSize = 16;

const styles = StyleSheet.create({
  container: { flex: 1, alignItems: "center", paddingTop: 30 },
  backdrop: { flex: 1, flexDirection: "column" },
  overlay: {
    paddingTop: 5,
    backgroundColor: "#000000",
    opacity: 0.5,
    flexDirection: "column",
    alignItems: "center"
  },
  row: {
    flexDirection: "row",
    flexWrap: "nowrap",
    alignItems: "flex-start",
    padding: 30
  },
  zipContainer: {
    height: baseFontSize + 10,
    borderBottomColor: "#DDDDDD",
    borderBottomWidth: 1,
    marginLeft: 5,
    marginTop: 3
  },
  zipCode: { flex: 1, flexBasis: 1, width: 50, height: baseFontSize },
  mainText: { fontSize: baseFontSize, color: "#FFFFFF" }
});

export default WeatherProject;
```

Now that we're done, try launching the application. It should work on both Android and iOS, in an emulator or on your physical device. What would you like to change or improve?

You can view the completed application in the GitHub repository (*https://github.com/bonniee/learning-react-native/tree/2.0.0/src/weather*).

Summary

For our first real application, we've already covered a lot of ground. We introduced a new UI component, <TextInput>, and learned how to use it to get information from the user. We demonstrated how to implement basic styling in React Native, as well as how to use images and include assets in our application. Finally, we learned how to use the React Native networking API to request data from external web sources. Not bad for a first application!

Hopefully, this chapter has demonstrated how quickly you can build React Native applications with useful features that feel at home on a mobile device.

If you want to extend your application further, here are some things to try:

- Add more images and change them based on the forecast
- Add validation to the zip code field
- Switch to using a more appropriate keypad for the zip code input
- Display the five-day weather forecast

Once we cover more topics, such as geolocation, you will be able to extend the weather application even further.

Of course, this has been a pretty quick survey. In the next few chapters, we will focus on gaining a deeper understanding of React Native best practices, and look at how to use a lot more features, too!

CHAPTER 4

Components for Mobile

In Chapter 3, we built a simple weather app. In doing so, we touched upon the basics of building interfaces with React Native. In this chapter, we will take a closer look at the mobile-based components used for React Native, and how they compare to basic HTML elements. Mobile interfaces are based on different primitive UI elements than web pages, and thus we need to use different components.

This chapter starts with a more detailed overview of the most basic components: `<View>`, `<Image>`, and `<Text>`. Then, we will discuss how touch and gestures factor into React Native components, and how to handle touch events. Next, we will cover higher-level components, such as the tab bars, navigators, and lists, which allow you to combine other views into standard mobile interface patterns.

Analogies Between HTML Elements and Native Components

When developing for the web, we make use of a variety of basic HTML elements. These include `<div>`, `<span>`, and `<img>`, as well as organizational elements such as `<ol>`, `<ul>`, and `<table>`. (We could include a consideration of elements such as `<audio>`, `<svg>`, `<canvas>`, and so on, but we'll ignore them for now.)

When dealing with React Native, we don't use these HTML elements, but we use a variety of components that are nearly analogous to them (Table 4-1).

Table 4-1. Analogous HTML and Native components

HTML	React Native
div	<View>
img	<Image>
span, p	<Text>
ul/ol, li	<FlatList>, child items

Although these elements serve roughly the same purposes, they are not interchangeable. Let's take a look at how these components work on mobile with React Native and how they differ from their browser-based counterparts.

Can I Share Code Between React Native and My Web App?

Out of the box, React Native supports rendering to Android and iOS. If you want to render web-compatible views with React Native, check out react-native-web (*https://github.com/necolas/react-native-web*).

Regardless of your approach, any JavaScript code—including React components—that doesn't render basic elements can be shared. So, if your business logic is isolated from your rendering code, you'll be able to reuse it.

The <Text> Component

Rendering text is a deceptively basic function; nearly any application will need to render text somewhere. However, text within the context of React Native and mobile development works differently from text rendering for the web.

When working with text in HTML, you can include raw text strings in a variety of elements. Furthermore, you can style them with child tags such as <strong> and <em>. So, you might end up with an HTML snippet that looks like this:

```
<p>The quick <em>brown</em> fox jumped over the lazy <strong>dog</strong>.</p>
```

In React Native, only <Text> components may have plain-text nodes as children. In other words, this is not valid:

```
<View>
   Text doesn't go here!
</View>
```

Instead, wrap your text in a <Text> component:

```
<View>
  <Text>This is OK!</Text>
</View>
```

When dealing with `<Text>` components in React Native, you no longer have access to subtags such as `<strong>` and `<em>`, though you can apply styles to achieve similar effects by using attributes such as `fontWeight` and `fontStyle`. Here's how you might achieve a similar effect by making use of inline styles:

```
<Text>
  The quick <Text style={{fontStyle: "italic"}}>brown</Text> fox
  jumped over the lazy <Text style={{fontWeight: "bold"}}>dog</Text>.
</Text>
```

This approach could quickly become verbose. You'll likely want to create styled components as a sort of shorthand when dealing with text, as shown in Example 4-1.

Example 4-1. Creating reusable components for styling text

```
const styles = StyleSheet.create({
  bold: {
      fontWeight: "bold"
  },
  italic: {
      fontStyle: "italic"
  }
});

class Strong extends Component {
  render() {
    return (
    <Text style={styles.bold}>
      {this.props.children}
    </Text>);
  }
}

class Em extends Component {
  render() {
    return (
    <Text style={styles.italic}>
      {this.props.children}
    </Text>);
  }
}
```

Once you have declared these styled components, you can freely make use of styled nesting. Now the React Native version looks quite similar to the HTML version (see Example 4-2).

Example 4-2. Using styled components for rendering text

```
<Text>
  The quick <Em>brown</Em> fox jumped
```

```
over the lazy <Strong>dog</Strong>.
</Text>
```

Similarly, React Native does not inherently have any concept of header elements (h1, h2, etc.), but it's easy to declare your own styled <Text> elements and use them as needed.

In general, when dealing with styled text, React Native forces you to change your approach. Style inheritance is limited, so you lose the ability to have default font settings for all text nodes in the tree. Once again, the React Native documentation recommends solving this by using styled components:

> You also lose the ability to set up a default font for an entire subtree. The recommended way to use consistent fonts and sizes across your application is to create a component MyAppText that includes them and use this component across your app. You can also use this component to make more specific components like MyAppHeader Text for other kinds of text.

The <Text> component documentation (*http://bit.ly/1SVQxU3*) has more details on this.

You've probably noticed a pattern here: React Native is very opinionated in its preference for reusing styled components over inheriting or reusing styles. While it can be time-consuming initially, this approach leads to better isolation so that you can render a component anywhere in your application and get the same result. This in turn makes it easier to maintain the styling code in your application. We'll discuss this approach further in the next chapter.

The <Image> Component

If text is *the* most basic element in an application, images are a close contender for both mobile and the web. When writing HTML and CSS for the web, we include images in a variety of ways: sometimes we use the <img> tag whereas at other times we apply images via CSS, such as when we use the background-image property. In React Native, we have a similar <Image> component, but it behaves a little differently.

The basic usage of the <Image> component is straightforward; just set the source prop:

```
<Image source={require("./puppies.png")} />
```

The image path is resolved exactly as JavaScript modules are resolved. So, in the preceding example, *puppies.png* should be provided in the same folder as the component that requires it.

There's some filename magic going on here, too. If you provide *puppies.ios.png* and *puppies.android.png*, the appropriate file will be rendered on each platform. Similarly, if you provide images with suffixes *@2x* and *@3x*, the React Native packager will select the appropriate image for the device's screen density.

It is also possible to include web-based image sources instead of bundling your assets with your application. For example:

```
<Image source={{uri: "https://facebook.github.io/react/img/logo_og.png"}}
       style={{width: 400, height: 400}} />
```

When utilizing network resources, you will need to specify dimensions manually.

Downloading images via the network rather than including them as assets has some advantages. During development, for instance, it may be easier to use this approach while prototyping rather than carefully importing all of your assets ahead of time. It also reduces the size of your bundled mobile application so that users do not need to download all of your assets. However, it means that instead you'll be relying on their data plan whenever they access your application in the future. For most cases, you'll want to avoid using the URI-based method.

If you're wondering about working with the user's own images, we'll cover the camera roll in Chapter 6.

Because React Native emphasizes a component-based approach, images *must* be included as <Image> components instead of being referenced via styles. For instance, in Chapter 3, we wanted to use an image as a background for our weather application. Whereas in plain HTML and CSS you would likely use the background-image property to apply a background image, in React Native you instead use the <Image> as a container component, like so:

```
<Image source={require("./puppies.png")}>
  {/* Your content here... */}
</Image>
```

Styling the images themselves is fairly straightforward. In addition to applying styles, you'll use certain props to control how the image will be rendered. You'll often make use of the resizeMode prop, for instance, which can be set to contain, cover, or stretch. The UIExplorer app demonstrates this well (Figure 4-1).

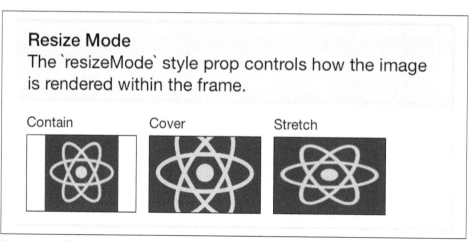

Resize Mode
The `resizeMode` style prop controls how the image is rendered within the frame.

Contain   Cover   Stretch

Figure 4-1. The difference between resize, cover, and contain

The <Image> component is very flexible. You will likely make extensive use of it in your own applications.

Working with Touch and Gestures

Web-based interfaces are usually designed for mouse-based controllers. We use things like hover state to indicate interactivity and respond to user interaction. For mobile, it's touch that matters. Mobile platforms have their own norms around interactions that you'll want to design for. This varies somewhat from platform to platform: iOS behaves differently from Android, which behaves differently yet again from Windows Phone.

React Native provides a number of APIs for you to leverage as you build touch-ready interfaces. In this section, we'll look at the humble <Button> component and the <TouchableHighlight> container component, as well as lower-level APIs that give you direct access to touch events.

Creating Basic Interactions with <Button>

If you're just getting started and need a basic, interactive button, the default <Button> component has you covered. It provides a simple API, which allows you to set the color, label text, and callback function.

```
<Button
  onPress={this._onPress}
  title="Press me"
  color="#841584"
  accessibilityLabel="Press this button"
/>
```

This `<Button>` component is a decent starting point, but you'll probably want to create your own interactive components. For that, we'll need to use `<TouchableHighlight>`.

Using the `<TouchableHighlight>` Component

Any interface elements that respond to user touch (buttons, control elements, etc.) should usually have a `<TouchableHighlight>` wrapper. `<TouchableHighlight>` causes an overlay to appear when the view is touched, giving the user visual feedback. This is one of the key interactions that causes a mobile application to feel *native*, as opposed to a mobile-optimized website, where touch feedback is limited. As a general rule of thumb, you should use `<TouchableHighlight>` anywhere there would be a button or a link on the web.

At its most basic usage, you just need to wrap your component in a `<TouchableHighlight>`, which will add a simple overlay when pressed. The `<TouchableHighlight>` component also gives you hooks for events such as `onPressIn`, `onPressOut`, `onLongPress`, and the like, so you can use these events in your React applications.

Example 4-3 shows how you can wrap a component in a `<TouchableHighlight>` in order to give the user feedback.

Example 4-3. Using the `<TouchableHighlight>` component

```
<TouchableHighlight
  onPressIn={this._onPressIn}
  onPressOut={this._onPressOut}
  accessibilityLabel={'PUSH ME'}
  style={styles.touchable}>
    <View style={styles.button}>
      <Text style={styles.welcome}>
        {this.state.pressing ? "EEK!" : "PUSH ME"}
      </Text>
    </View>
</TouchableHighlight>
```

When the user taps the button, an overlay appears, and the text changes (Figure 4-2).

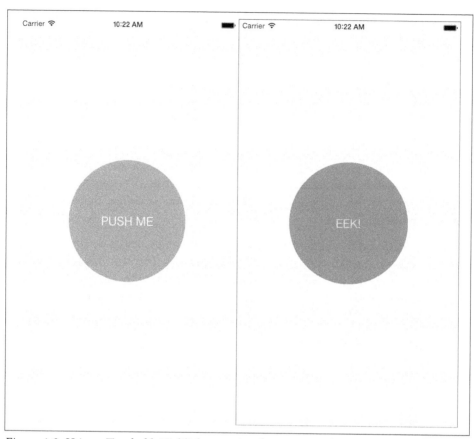

Figure 4-2. Using <TouchableHighlight> to give the user visual feedback—the unpressed state (left) and the pressed state, with highlight (right)

This is a contrived example, but it illustrates the basic interactions that make a button "feel" touchable on mobile. The overlay is a key piece of feedback that informs the user that an element can be pressed. Note that in order to apply the overlay, we don't need to apply any logic to our styles; the <TouchableHighlight> handles the logic of that for us.

Example 4-4 shows the full code for this button component.

Example 4-4. PressDemo.js illustrates the use of <TouchableHighlight>

```
import React, { Component } from "react";
import { StyleSheet, Text, View, TouchableHighlight } from "react-native";

class Button extends Component {
  constructor(props) {
    super(props);
```

```
    this.state = { pressing: false };
  }

  _onPressIn = () => {
    this.setState({ pressing: true });
  };

  _onPressOut = () => {
    this.setState({ pressing: false });
  };

  render() {
    return (
      <View style={styles.container}>
        <TouchableHighlight
          onPressIn={this._onPressIn}
          onPressOut={this._onPressOut}
          style={styles.touchable}
        >

          <View style={styles.button}>
            <Text style={styles.welcome}>
              {this.state.pressing ? "EEK!" : "PUSH ME"}
            </Text>
          </View>

        </TouchableHighlight>
      </View>
    );
  }
}

const styles = StyleSheet.create({
  container: {
    flex: 1,
    justifyContent: "center",
    alignItems: "center",
    backgroundColor: "#F5FCFF"
  },
  welcome: { fontSize: 20, textAlign: "center", margin: 10, color: "#FFFFFF" },
  touchable: { borderRadius: 100 },
  button: {
    backgroundColor: "#FF0000",
    borderRadius: 100,
    height: 200,
    width: 200,
    justifyContent: "center"
  }
});

export default Button;
```

Try editing this button to respond to other events, by using hooks like `onPress` and `onLongPress`. The best way to get a sense for how these events map onto user interactions is to experiment using a real device.

Using the PanResponder Class

Unlike `<TouchableHighlight>`, PanResponder is not a component but rather a class provided by React Native. A PanResponder `gestureState` object gives you access to raw position data as well as information such as velocity and accumulated distance of the current gesture.

To make use of `PanResponder` in a React component, we need to create a `PanResponder` object and then attach it to a component's `render` method.

Creating a `PanResponder` requires us to specify the proper handlers for `PanResponder` events (Example 4-5).

Example 4-5. Creating a PanResponder requires us to register several callbacks

```
this._panResponder = PanResponder.create({
  onStartShouldSetPanResponder: this._handleStartShouldSetPanResponder,
  onMoveShouldSetPanResponder: this._handleMoveShouldSetPanResponder,
  onPanResponderGrant: this._handlePanResponderGrant,
  onPanResponderMove: this._handlePanResponderMove,
  onPanResponderRelease: this._handlePanResponderEnd,
  onPanResponderTerminate: this._handlePanResponderEnd,
});
```

These six functions give us access to the full lifecycle of a touch event. `onStartShould SetPanResponder` and `onMoveShouldSetPanResponder` determine whether or not we should respond to a given touch event. `onPanResponderGrant` will be invoked when a touch event begins, and `onPanResponderRelease` and `onPanResponderTerminate` will be invoked when a touch event ends. We'll be able to access data about the ongoing touch event during `onPanResponderMove`.

We use spread syntax to attach the `PanResponder` to the view in our component's `render` method (Example 4-6).

Example 4-6. Attaching the PanResponder using spread sytax

```
render: function() {
  return (
    <View
      {...this._panResponder.panHandlers}>
      { /* View contents here */ }
    </View>
```

```
    );
}
```

After this, the handlers that you passed to the `PanResponder.create` call will be invoked during the appropriate move events if the touch originates within this view.

Figure 4-3 renders a circle that you can drag around the screen. Its coordinates will be updated as you move it.

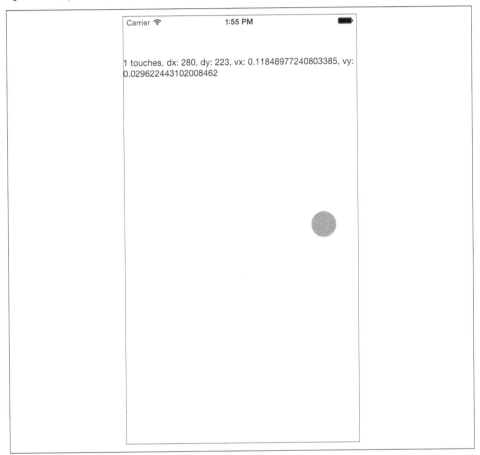

Figure 4-3. PanResponder demo

In order to implement this, let's flesh out our `PanResponder` callbacks now. The first two are straightforward: by implementing `_handleStartShouldSetPanResponder` and `_handleMoveShouldSetPanResponder`, we can declare that we want this responder to receive touch events (Example 4-7).

Example 4-7. For the first two callbacks, we simply return true

```
_handleStartShouldSetPanResponder = (event, gestureState) => {
  // Should we become active when the user presses down on the circle?
  return true;
};

_handleMoveShouldSetPanResponder = (event, gestureState) => {
  // Should we become active when the user moves a touch over the circle?
  return true;
};
```

Then we'll want to use the location data in _handlePanResponderMove to update the coordinates of our circle view (Example 4-8).

Example 4-8. Updating the circle's position in _handlePanResponderMove

```
_handlePanResponderMove = (event, gestureState) => {
  // Calculate current position using deltas
  this._circleStyles.style.left = this._previousLeft + gestureState.dx;
  this._circleStyles.style.top = this._previousTop + gestureState.dy;
  this._updatePosition();
};

_updatePosition = () => {
  this.circle && this.circle.setNativeProps(this._circleStyles);
};
```

Note that we're calling setNativeProps here in order to update the position of the circle view.

 When working with animations, you can use setNativeProps to directly modify a component instead of the typical approach of setting state and props. This lets you bypass the overhead of rerendering the component hierarchy, but it should be used sparingly.

Next, let's implement _handlePanResponderGrant and _handlePanResponderEnd so that the circle changes color when a touch is active (Example 4-9).

Example 4-9. Implementing highlight behavior

```
_highlight = () => {
  this.circle &&
    this.circle.setNativeProps({
      style: { backgroundColor: "blue" }
    });
};
```

```
_unHighlight = () => {
  this.circle &&
    this.circle.setNativeProps({ style: { backgroundColor: "green" } });
};

_handlePanResponderGrant = (event, gestureState) => {
  this._highlight();
};

_handlePanResponderEnd = (event, gestureState) => {
  this._unHighlight();
};
```

Let's put it all together to build an interactive view using `PanResponder`, as shown in Example 4-10.

Example 4-10. PanDemo.js illustrates the use of PanResponder

```
// Adapted from https://github.com/facebook/react-native/blob/master/
// Examples/UIExplorer/PanResponderExample.js

"use strict";

import React, { Component } from "react";
import { StyleSheet, PanResponder, View, Text } from "react-native";

const CIRCLE_SIZE = 40;
const CIRCLE_COLOR = "blue";
const CIRCLE_HIGHLIGHT_COLOR = "green";

class PanResponderExample extends Component {
  // Set some initial values.
  _panResponder = {};
  _previousLeft = 0;
  _previousTop = 0;
  _circleStyles = {};
  circle = null;

  constructor(props) {
    super(props);
    this.state = {
      numberActiveTouches: 0,
      moveX: 0,
      moveY: 0,
      x0: 0,
      y0: 0,
      dx: 0,
      dy: 0,
      vx: 0,
      vy: 0
```

```
    };
  }

  componentWillMount() {
    this._panResponder = PanResponder.create({
      onStartShouldSetPanResponder: this._handleStartShouldSetPanResponder,
      onMoveShouldSetPanResponder: this._handleMoveShouldSetPanResponder,
      onPanResponderGrant: this._handlePanResponderGrant,
      onPanResponderMove: this._handlePanResponderMove,
      onPanResponderRelease: this._handlePanResponderEnd,
      onPanResponderTerminate: this._handlePanResponderEnd
    });
    this._previousLeft = 20;
    this._previousTop = 84;
    this._circleStyles = {
      style: { left: this._previousLeft, top: this._previousTop }
    };
  }

  componentDidMount() {
    this._updatePosition();
  }

  render() {
    return (
      <View style={styles.container}>
        <View
          ref={circle => {
            this.circle = circle;
          }}
          style={styles.circle}
          {...this._panResponder.panHandlers}
        />
        <Text>
          {this.state.numberActiveTouches} touches,
          dx: {this.state.dx},
          dy: {this.state.dy},
          vx: {this.state.vx},
          vy: {this.state.vy}
        </Text>
      </View>
    );
  }

  // _highlight and _unHighlight get called by PanResponder methods,
  // providing visual feedback to the user.
  _highlight = () => {
    this.circle &&
      this.circle.setNativeProps({
        style: { backgroundColor: CIRCLE_HIGHLIGHT_COLOR }
      });
  };
```

```
_unHighlight = () => {
  this.circle &&
    this.circle.setNativeProps({ style: { backgroundColor: CIRCLE_COLOR } });
};

// We're controlling the circle's position directly with setNativeProps.
_updatePosition = () => {
  this.circle && this.circle.setNativeProps(this._circleStyles);
};

_handleStartShouldSetPanResponder = (event, gestureState) => {
  // Should we become active when the user presses down on the circle?
  return true;
};

_handleMoveShouldSetPanResponder = (event, gestureState) => {
  // Should we become active when the user moves a touch over the circle?
  return true;
};

_handlePanResponderGrant = (event, gestureState) => {
  this._highlight();
};

_handlePanResponderMove = (event, gestureState) => {
  this.setState({
    stateID: gestureState.stateID,
    moveX: gestureState.moveX,
    moveY: gestureState.moveY,
    x0: gestureState.x0,
    y0: gestureState.y0,
    dx: gestureState.dx,
    dy: gestureState.dy,
    vx: gestureState.vx,
    vy: gestureState.vy,
    numberActiveTouches: gestureState.numberActiveTouches
  });

  // Calculate current position using deltas
  this._circleStyles.style.left = this._previousLeft + gestureState.dx;
  this._circleStyles.style.top = this._previousTop + gestureState.dy;
  this._updatePosition();
};

_handlePanResponderEnd = (event, gestureState) => {
  this._unHighlight();
  this._previousLeft += gestureState.dx;
  this._previousTop += gestureState.dy;
};
}
```

```
const styles = StyleSheet.create({
  circle: {
    width: CIRCLE_SIZE,
    height: CIRCLE_SIZE,
    borderRadius: CIRCLE_SIZE / 2,
    backgroundColor: CIRCLE_COLOR,
    position: "absolute",
    left: 0,
    top: 0
  },
  container: { flex: 1, paddingTop: 64 }
});

export default PanResponderExample;
```

If you plan on implementing your own gesture recognizers, I suggest experimenting with this application on a real device so that you can get a feel for how these values respond. Figure 4-3 shows a screenshot, but you'll want to experience it on a device with a real touchscreen.

Choosing how to handle touch

How should you decide when to use the touch and gesture APIs discussed in this section? It depends on what you want to build.

In order to provide the user with basic feedback and indicate that a button or another element is "tappable," use the `<TouchableHighlight>` component.

In order to implement your own custom touch interfaces, you can use `PanResponder`. If you are designing a game, or an application with an unusual interface, you'll need to spend some time building out the custom touch interactions you want.

For many applications, you won't need to implement any custom touch handling. In the next section, we'll look at some of the higher-level components that implement common UI patterns for you.

Working with Lists

Many mobile user interfaces feature lists as a central element. You can see this interaction pattern in the Dropbox, Twitter, and iOS Settings apps (Figure 4-4). At its heart, a list is just a scrolling container with some child views. This deceptively simple design pattern is integral to many mobile interfaces.

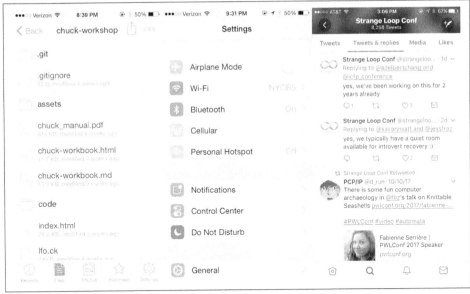

Figure 4-4. Lists as used by Dropbox, Twitter, and the iOS Settings app

React Native provides two list components with convenient APIs. The `<FlatList>` component is designed to work with long scrolling lists of changing but similarly structured data. It has several performance optimizations baked in. The `<Section List>` component is designed for data that is broken into logical sections, usually with section headings, similar to the iOS `UITableView`. Together, `<FlatList>` and `<SectionList>` cover most common use cases but if you need to peek under the hood and add some custom list handling, take a look at `<VirtualizedList>`.

Optimizing list-rendering performance is a notoriously tricky problem because different use cases call for different approaches. Is your user swiping hastily through a contacts list to find a particular person or are they slowly perusing a feed of images? Do you have a homogeneous list or is every child view different? If you hit performance issues, pay attention to your lists.

In this section, we are going to build an app that displays the *New York Times* Best Sellers list and lets us view data about each book, as shown in Figure 4-5. We'll build two versions, one with `<FlatList>` and the other with `<SectionList>`.

If you'd like, you can grab your own API token from the *New York Times* (*http://devel oper.nytimes.com/apps/mykeys*). Otherwise, use the API token included in the sample code.

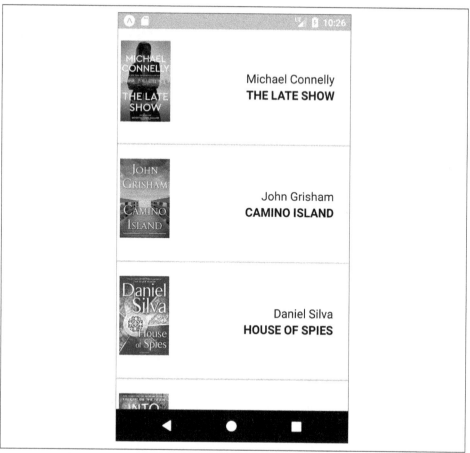

Figure 4-5. The BookList application we'll be building

Using the Basic <FlatList> Component

We're going to start with the basic `<FlatList>` component, which requires two props: `data` and `renderItem`.

```
<FlatList
  data={this.state.data}
  renderItem={this._renderItem} />
```

`data` is, as the name implies, the data that your `<FlatList>` will render. It should be an array where each element has a unique key property, plus whatever other properties you find useful.

`renderItem` should be a function that returns a component based on the data from one element of the `data` array.

The basic usage of a `<FlatList>` is demonstrated in Example 4-11.

Example 4-11. src/bestsellers/SimpleList.js

```
import React, { Component } from "react";

import { StyleSheet, Text, View, FlatList } from "react-native";

class SimpleList extends Component {
  constructor(props) {
    super(props);
    this.state = {
      data: [
        { key: "a" },
        { key: "b" },
        { key: "c" },
        { key: "d" },
        { key: "a longer example" },
        { key: "e" },
        { key: "f" },
        { key: "g" },
        { key: "h" },
        { key: "i" },
        { key: "j" },
        { key: "k" },
        { key: "l" },
        { key: "m" },
        { key: "n" },
        { key: "o" },
        { key: "p" }
      ]
    };
  }

  _renderItem = data => {
    return <Text style={styles.row}>{data.item.key}</Text>;
  };

  render() {
    return (
      <View style={styles.container}>
        <FlatList data={this.state.data} renderItem={this._renderItem} />
      </View>
    );
  }
}

const styles = StyleSheet.create({
  container: {
    flex: 1,
    justifyContent: "center",
```

```
    alignItems: "center",
    backgroundColor: "#F5FCFF"
  },
  row: { fontSize: 24, padding: 42, borderWidth: 1, borderColor: "#DDDDDD" }
});
```

```
export default SimpleList;
```

One of the common "gotchas" of working with <FlatList> is that renderItem gets
passed an object with the actual data accessible via the item property.

```
_renderItem = data => {
  return <Text style={styles.row}>{data.item.key}</Text>;
};
```

We could simplify this with destructuring shorthand:

```
_renderItem = ({item}) => {
  return <Text style={styles.row}>{item.key}</Text>;
};
```

The app should look like Figure 4-6.

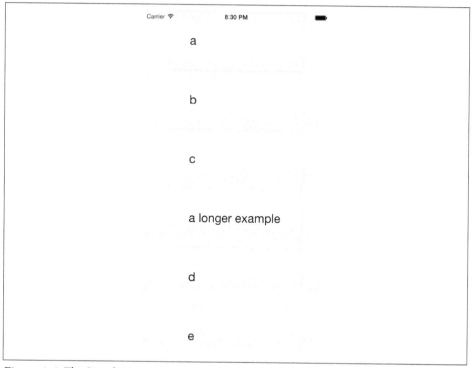

Figure 4-6. The SimpleList component renders a bare-bones <FlatList>

Updating the <FlatList> Contents

What if we want to do something a little more interesting? Let's create a <FlatList> with more complex data. We will be using the New York Times API to create a simple Best Sellers application, which renders the *New York Times* Best Sellers list.

To begin with, we'll use fake data to represent an example response from the New York Times API, as shown in Example 4-12.

Example 4-12. Mock data based on the expected API response

```
const mockBooks = [
  {
    rank: 1,
    title: "GATHERING PREY",
    author: "John Sandford",
    book_image:
      "http://du.ec2.nytimes.com.s3.amazonaws.com/prd/books/9780399168796.jpg"
  },
  {
    rank: 2,
    title: "MEMORY MAN",
    author: "David Baldacci",
    book_image:
      "http://du.ec2.nytimes.com.s3.amazonaws.com/prd/books/9781455586387.jpg"
  }
];
```

Then we'll add a component that can render this data. The <BookItem> component, shown in Example 4-13, uses a combination of <View>, <Text>, and <Image> to display basic information about each book.

Example 4-13. src/bestsellers/BookItem.js

```
import React, { Component } from "react";

import { StyleSheet, Text, View, Image, ListView } from "react-native";

const styles = StyleSheet.create({
  bookItem: {
    flexDirection: "row",
    backgroundColor: "#FFFFFF",
    borderBottomColor: "#AAAAAA",
    borderBottomWidth: 2,
    padding: 5,
    height: 175
  },
  cover: { flex: 1, height: 150, resizeMode: "contain" },
  info: {
```

```
      flex: 3,
      alignItems: "flex-end",
      flexDirection: "column",
      alignSelf: "center",
      padding: 20
   },
   author: { fontSize: 18 },
   title: { fontSize: 18, fontWeight: "bold" }
});

class BookItem extends Component {
   render() {
      return (
         <View style={styles.bookItem}>
           <Image style={styles.cover} source= />
           <View style={styles.info}>
             <Text style={styles.author}>{this.props.author}</Text>
             <Text style={styles.title}>{this.props.title}</Text>
           </View>
         </View>
      );
   }
}

export default BookItem;
```

In order to use the <BookItem> component, we need to update our _renderItem
function. A <BookItem> expects three props: coverURL, title, and author.

```
   _renderItem = ({ item }) => {
      return (
         <BookItem
           coverURL={item.book_image}
           title={item.key}
           author={item.author}
         />
      );
   };
```

Remember that in a <FlatList>, each element in the data array must have a unique
key property defined. So, we'll add a helper method that takes an array of objects and
adds a key property to them, as shown in Example 4-14.

*Example 4-14. The _addKeysToBooks method adds a key to each object in the books
array*

```
_addKeysToBooks = books => {
  return books.map(book => {
    return Object.assign(book, { key: book.title });
  });
};
```

Now that we have this helper method, we can update our initial state using the mock data from Example 4-12:

```
constructor(props) {
  super(props);
  this.state = { data: this._addKeysToBooks(mockBooks) };
}
```

Once we put it all together, our mocked-out Best Sellers application code should look like Example 4-15, with the resulting app displayed in Figure 4-7.

Example 4-15. src/bestsellers/MockBookList.js

```javascript
import React, { Component } from "react";

import { StyleSheet, Text, View, Image, FlatList } from "react-native";

import BookItem from "./BookItem";

const mockBooks = [
  {
    rank: 1,
    title: "GATHERING PREY",
    author: "John Sandford",
    book_image:
      "http://du.ec2.nytimes.com.s3.amazonaws.com/prd/books/9780399168796.jpg"
  },
  {
    rank: 2,
    title: "MEMORY MAN",
    author: "David Baldacci",
    book_image:
      "http://du.ec2.nytimes.com.s3.amazonaws.com/prd/books/9781455586387.jpg"
  }
];

class BookList extends Component {
  constructor(props) {
    super(props);
    this.state = { data: this._addKeysToBooks(mockBooks) };
  }

  _renderItem = ({ item }) => {
    return (
      <BookItem
        coverURL={item.book_image}
        title={item.key}
        author={item.author}
      />
    );
  };
```

```
  _addKeysToBooks = books => {
    // Takes the API response from the NYTimes
    // and adds a key property to the object
    // for rendering purposes
    return books.map(book => {
      return Object.assign(book, { key: book.title });
    });
  };

  render() {
    return <FlatList data={this.state.data} renderItem={this._renderItem} />;
  }
}

const styles = StyleSheet.create({ container: { flex: 1, paddingTop: 22 } });

export default BookList;
```

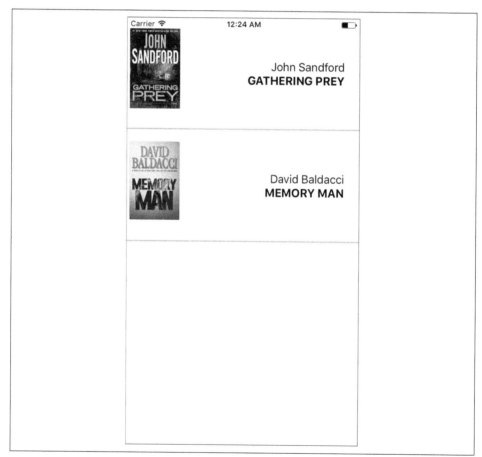

Figure 4-7. Mock data displayed using <FlatList>

Integrating Real Data

Hardcoded data is well and good, but let's test the real thing. The actual code to access the New York Times API is provided in Example 4-16.

Example 4-16. src/bestsellers/NYT.js

```
const API_KEY = "73b19491b83909c7e07016f4bb4644f9:2:60667290";
const LIST_NAME = "hardcover-fiction";
const API_STEM = "https://api.nytimes.com/svc/books/v3/lists";

function fetchBooks(list_name = LIST_NAME) {
  let url = `${API_STEM}/${LIST_NAME}?response-format=json&api-key=${API_KEY}`;
  return fetch(url)
    .then(response => response.json())
    .then(responseJson => {
      return responseJson.results.books;
    })
    .catch(error => {
      console.error(error);
    });
}

export default { fetchBooks: fetchBooks };
```

Let's import that library into our component now.

```
import NYT from "./NYT";
```

Now let's add a `_refreshData` method that invokes the New York Times API:

```
_refreshData = () => {
  NYT.fetchBooks().then(books => {
    this.setState({ data: this._addKeysToBooks(books) });
  });
};
```

Finally, we need to set our initial state to an empty array and call `_refreshData` in `componentDidMount`. Once we do that, our application will render live data from the *New York Times* Best Sellers list! The full code is shown in Example 4-17, and you can see the updated app in Figure 4-8.

Example 4-17. src/bestsellers/BookList.js

```
import React, { Component } from "react";

import { StyleSheet, Text, View, Image, FlatList } from "react-native";

import BookItem from "./BookItem";
import NYT from "./NYT";
```

```
class BookList extends Component {
  constructor(props) {
    super(props);
    this.state = { data: [] };
  }

  componentDidMount() {
    this._refreshData();
  }

  _renderItem = ({ item }) => {
    return (
      <BookItem
        coverURL={item.book_image}
        title={item.key}
        author={item.author}
      />
    );
  };

  _addKeysToBooks = books => {
    // Takes the API response from the NYTimes
    // and adds a key property to the object
    // for rendering purposes
    return books.map(book => {
      return Object.assign(book, { key: book.title });
    });
  };

  _refreshData = () => {
    NYT.fetchBooks().then(books => {
      this.setState({ data: this._addKeysToBooks(books) });
    });
  };

  render() {
    return (
      <View style={styles.container}>
        <FlatList data={this.state.data} renderItem={this._renderItem} />
      </View>
    );
  }
}

const styles = StyleSheet.create({ container: { flex: 1, paddingTop: 22 } });

export default BookList;
```

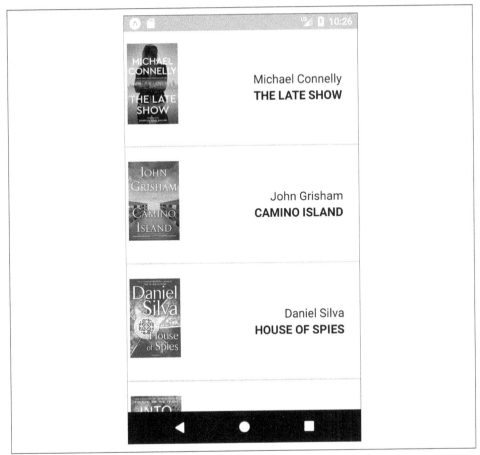

Figure 4-8. Viewing current best sellers, with <FlatList>

As you can see, working with the <FlatList> component is straightforward as long as you remember to structure your data properly. In addition to handling scrolling and touch interactions, <FlatList> also includes many performance optimizations to speed up rendering and reduce memory usage.

Working with <SectionList>

The <SectionList> component is designed for data sets where you have mostly homogeneous items plus optional section headings. For example, if we wanted to render several different kinds of best sellers lists with headings between them, a <SectionList> would be a good choice.

A <SectionList> expects the props sections, renderItem, and renderSection Header. We'll start with sections, which should be an array where each object contains section data. Each section object must have the `title` and `data` keys. The `data` must look similar to `data` in a `<FlatList>`: it should be an array where each element has a unique key property.

Let's update our `_renderData` method to fetch both the fiction and nonfiction best sellers lists, and update our component's state accordingly.

```
_refreshData = () => {
  Promise
    .all([
      NYT.fetchBooks("hardcover-fiction"),
      NYT.fetchBooks("hardcover-nonfiction")
    ])
    .then(results => {
      if (results.length !== 2) {
        console.error("Unexpected results");
      }

      this.setState({
        sections: [
          {
            title: "Hardcover Fiction",
            data: this._addKeysToBooks(results[0])
          },
          {
            title: "Hardcover NonFiction",
            data: this._addKeysToBooks(results[1])
          }
        ]
      });
    });
};
```

We don't need to update our `_renderItem` method, but we do need to add a new `_renderHeader` method. Let's do that next.

```
_renderHeader = ({ section }) => {
  return (
    <Text style={styles.headingText}>
      {section.title}
    </Text>
  );
};
```

Finally, we need to update our `render` method to return a `<SectionList>` instead of a `<FlatList>`.

```
<SectionList
  sections={this.state.sections}
  renderItem={this._renderItem}
  renderSectionHeader={this._renderHeader}
/>
```

When we put everything together, our usage of <SectionList> should look like Example 4-18, resulting in the updated app shown in Figure 4-9.

Example 4-18. src/bestsellers/BookSectionList.js

```
import React, { Component } from "react";

import { StyleSheet, Text, View, Image, SectionList } from "react-native";

import BookItem from "./BookItem";
import NYT from "./NYT";

class BookList extends Component {
  constructor(props) {
    super(props);
    this.state = { sections: [] };
  }

  componentDidMount() {
    this._refreshData();
  }

  _addKeysToBooks = books => {
    // Takes the API response from the NYTimes
    // and adds a key property to the object
    // for rendering purposes
    return books.map(book => {
      return Object.assign(book, { key: book.title });
    });
  };

  _refreshData = () => {
    Promise
      .all([
        NYT.fetchBooks("hardcover-fiction"),
        NYT.fetchBooks("hardcover-nonfiction")
      ])
      .then(results => {
        if (results.length !== 2) {
          console.error("Unexpected results");
        }

        this.setState({
          sections: [
            {
              title: "Hardcover Fiction",
              data: this._addKeysToBooks(results[0])
            },
            {
              title: "Hardcover NonFiction",
              data: this._addKeysToBooks(results[1])
```

```
              }
            ]
          });
        });
    };

    _renderItem = ({ item }) => {
      return (
        <BookItem
          coverURL={item.book_image}
          title={item.key}
          author={item.author}
        />
      );
    };

    _renderHeader = ({ section }) => {
      return (
        <Text style={styles.headingText}>
          {section.title}
        </Text>
      );
    };

    render() {
      return (
        <View style={styles.container}>
          <SectionList
            sections={this.state.sections}
            renderItem={this._renderItem}
            renderSectionHeader={this._renderHeader}
          />
        </View>
      );
    }
  }

const styles = StyleSheet.create({
  container: { flex: 1, paddingTop: 22 },
  headingText: {
    fontSize: 24,
    alignSelf: "center",
    backgroundColor: "#FFF",
    fontWeight: "bold",
    paddingLeft: 20,
    paddingRight: 20,
    paddingTop: 2,
    paddingBottom: 2
  }
});

export default BookList;
```

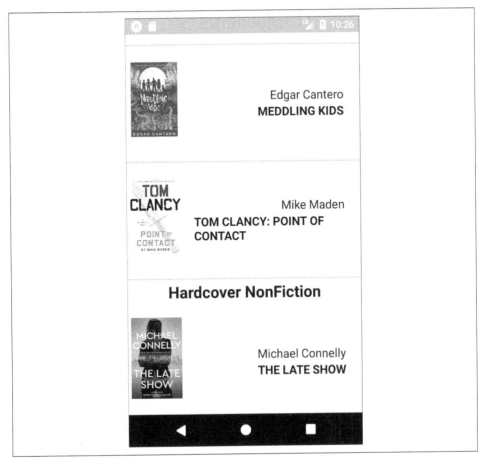

Figure 4-9. Viewing current best sellers, with <SectionList>

Navigation

Navigation in the context of mobile apps refers, roughly, to the code that allows users to transition from one screen to another. On the web, this is part of the window.his tory API, which provides concepts such as "backward" and "forward."

Commonly used components for navigation in React Native include the built-in <Navigator> and <NavigatorIOS> components, as well as community solutions like <StackNavigator> (provided by the react-navigation library).

Navigation logic is necessary in order to move between screens in your mobile application. It also enables "deep linking," so that users can jump from a URL into a particular screen within your app.

We'll cover navigation in depth in Chapter 10.

Other Organizational Components

There are plenty of other organizational components, too. A few useful ones include `<TabBarIOS>` and `<SegmentedControlIOS>` (illustrated in Figure 4-10) and `<Drawer LayoutAndroid>` and `<ToolbarAndroid>` (illustrated in Figure 4-11).

You'll notice that these are all named with platform-specific suffixes. That's because they wrap native APIs for platform-specific UI elements.

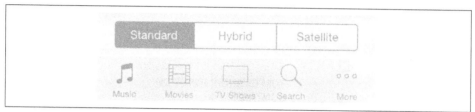

Figure 4-10. An iOS segmented control (top) and an iOS tab bar (bottom)

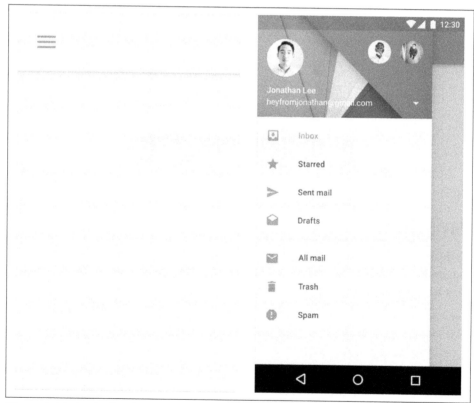

Figure 4-11. An Android toolbar (left) and an Android drawer (right)

These components are very useful for organizing multiple screens within your application. <TabBarIOS> and <DrawerLayoutAndroid>, for example, give you an easy way to switch between multiple modes or functions. <SegmentedControlIOS> and <ToolbarAndroid> are better suited for more fine-grained controls.

You'll want to refer to the platform-specific design guidelines for how best to use these components:

- Android Design Guide (*http://bit.ly/android_design_guide*)
- iOS Human Interface Guidelines (*http://bit.ly/designing_for_ios*)

We'll cover how to use platform-specific components in more depth in Chapter 7.

Summary

In this chapter, we dug into the specifics of a variety of the most important components in React Native. We discussed how to use basic low-level components, like <Text> and <Image>, as well as more abstract components like <FlatList>, <SectionList>, and <TabBarIOS>. We also looked at how to use various touch-focused APIs and components in case you want to build your own custom touch handlers.

At this point, you should be equipped to build basic functional applications using React Native! Now that you've acquainted yourself with the components discussed in this chapter, building upon them and combining them to create your own applications should feel remarkably similar to working with React on the web.

Of course, building up basic functioning applications is only part of the battle. In the next chapter, we'll focus on styling and how to use React Native's implementation of styles to get the look and feel you want on mobile.

Styles

It's great to be able to build functional applications, but if you can't style them effectively, you won't get very far! In Chapter 3, we built a simple weather application with some basic styles. While this gave us an overview of how to style React Native components, we glossed over many of the details. In this chapter, we will take a closer look at how styles work in React Native. We'll cover how to create and manage your stylesheets, as well as the details of React Native's implementation of CSS rules. By the end of this chapter, you should feel comfortable creating and styling your own React Native components and applications.

If you want to share styles between your React Native and web applications, the React Style project on GitHub (*https://github.com/js-next/react-style*) provides a version of React Native's style system for the web.

Declaring and Manipulating Styles

When working with React for the web, we typically use separate stylesheet files, which may be written in CSS, SASS, or LESS. React Native takes a radically different approach, bringing styles entirely into the world of JavaScript and forcing you to link style objects explicitly to components. This approach tends to provoke strong reactions, as it represents a significant departure from CSS-based styling norms.

To understand the design of React Native's styles, first we need to consider some of the headaches associated with traditional CSS stylesheets.[1] CSS has a number of problems. All CSS rules and class names are global in scope, meaning that styling one component can easily break another if you're not careful. For instance, if you include

---

[1] The "CSS in JS" slidedeck (*https://speakerdeck.com/vjeux/react-css-in-js*) from Christopher Chedeau, aka Vjeux, provides a good overview.

the popular Twitter Bootstrap library, you will introduce over 600 new global variables. Because CSS is not explicitly connected to the HTML elements it styles, dead code elimination is difficult, and it can be nontrivial to determine which styles will apply to a given element.

Languages like SASS and LESS attempt to work around some of CSS's uglier parts, but many of the same fundamental problems remain. With React, we have the opportunity to keep the desirable parts of CSS, but also the freedom for significant divergence. React Native implements a subset of the available CSS styles, focusing on keeping the styling API narrow yet still highly expressive. Positioning is dramatically different, as we'll see later in this chapter. Additionally, React Native does not support pseudoclasses, animations, or selectors. A full list of supported properties can be found in the docs (*https://facebook.github.io/react-native/docs/view.html#style*).

Instead of stylesheets, in React Native we work with JavaScript-based style *objects*. One of React's greatest strengths is that it forces you to keep your JavaScript code—your components—modular. By bringing styles into the realm of JavaScript, React Native pushes us to write modular styles, too.

In this section, we'll cover the mechanics of how these style objects are created and manipulated in React Native.

Using Inline Styles

Inline styles are the simplest way, syntactically, to style a component in React Native, though they are not usually the *best* way. As you can see in Example 5-1, the syntax for inline styles in React Native is the same as for React for the browser.

Example 5-1. Using inline styles

```
<Text>
  The quick <Text style={{fontStyle: "italic"}}>brown</Text> fox
  jumped over the lazy <Text style={{fontWeight: "bold"}}>dog</Text>.
</Text>
```

Inline styles have some advantages. They're quick and dirty, allowing you to rapidly experiment.

However, you should avoid them in general because they're less efficient. Inline style objects must be recreated during each render pass. Even when you want to modify styles in response to props or state, you don't need to use inline styles, as we'll see in a moment.

Styling with Objects

If you take a look at the inline style syntax, you will see that it's simply passing an object to the `style` attribute. There's no need to create the style object in the `render` method, though. Instead, you can separate it out, as shown in Example 5-2.

Example 5-2. The style attribute will accept a JavaScript object

```
const italic = {
  fontStyle: "italic"
};
const bold = {
  fontWeight: "bold"
};

...

render() {
  return (
    <Text>
      The quick <Text style={italic}>brown</Text> fox
      jumped over the lazy <Text style={bold}>dog</Text>.
    </Text>
    );
}
```

Using StyleSheet.create

You will notice that almost all of the React Native example code makes use of `Style Sheet.create`. This function is a small piece of syntactic sugar with some added perks.

Creating StyleSheets rather than passing around raw JavaScript objects can reduce the number of allocations (thus benefiting performance); it also encourages you to organize your code more cleanly. These StyleSheets are immutable, which is usually helpful.

Using `StyleSheet.create` is strictly optional, but in general you'll want to use it.

PanDemo.js, from Example 4-10, gives us a good counterexample in which the immutability provided by `StyleSheet.create` is a hindrance rather than a help. Recall that we wanted to update the location of a circle based on movement—in other words, each time we received an update from the `PanResponder`, we needed to update state as well as change the styles on the circle. In this circumstance, we don't want immutability at all, at least not for the style controlling the circle's location. Therefore, we can use a plain object to store the style for the circle.

Concatenating Styles

What happens if you want to combine two or more styles?

Recall that earlier we said that we should prefer reusing styled components over styles. That's true, but sometimes style reuse is also useful. For instance, if you have a button style and an accentText style, you may want to combine them to create an AccentButton component.

If the styles look like this:

```
const styles = StyleSheet.create({
  button: {
    borderRadius: "8px",
    backgroundColor: "#99CCFF"
  },
  accentText: {
    fontSize: 18,
    fontWeight: "bold"
  }
});
```

Then you can create a component that has *both* of those styles applied through simple concatenation (Example 5-3).

Example 5-3. The style attribute also accepts an array of objects

```
class AccentButton extends Component {
  render() {
    return (
      <Text style={[styles.button, styles.accentText]}>
        {this.props.children}
      </Text>
    );
  }
}
```

As you can see, the style attribute can take an array of style objects. You can also add inline styles here if you want (Example 5-4).

Example 5-4. You can mix style objects and inline styles

```
class AccentButton extends Component {
  render() {
    return (
      <Text style={[styles.button, styles.accentText, {color: "#FFFFFF"}]}>
        {this.props.children}
      </Text>
    );
```

```
    }
}
```

In the case of a conflict, such as when two objects specify the same property, React Native will resolve the conflict for you. The rightmost elements in the style array take precedence, and false values (`false`, `null`, `undefined`) are ignored.

You can leverage this pattern to apply conditional styles. For example, if we had a `<Button>` component and wanted to apply extra style rules if it's being touched, we could use the code shown in Example 5-5.

Example 5-5. Using conditional styles

```
<View style={[styles.button, this.state.touching && styles.highlight]} />
```

This shortcut can help you keep your rendering logic concise.

In general, style concatenation is a useful tool for combining styles. It's interesting to contrast concatenation with web-based stylesheet approaches: @extend in SASS, or nesting and overriding classes in vanilla CSS. Style concatenation is a more limited tool, which is arguably a good thing: it keeps the logic simple and makes it easier to reason about which styles are being applied and how.

Organization and Inheritance

In most of the examples so far, we append our style code to the end of the main Java‐Script file with a single call to `StyleSheet.create`. For example code, this works well enough, but it's not something you'll likely want to do in an actual application. How should we actually organize styles? In this section, we will take a look at ways of organizing your styles, and how to share and inherit styles.

Exporting Style Objects

As your styles grow more complex, you will want to keep them separate from your components' JavaScript files. One common approach is to have a separate folder for each component. If you have a component named `<ComponentName>`, you would cre‐ate a folder named *ComponentName/* and structure it like so:

```
- ComponentName
  |- index.js
  |- styles.js
```

Within *styles.js*, you create a stylesheet and export it (Example 5-6).

Example 5-6. Exporting styles from a JavaScript file

```
import { StyleSheet } from "react-native";

const styles = StyleSheet.create({
  text: {
    color: "#FF00FF",
    fontSize: 16
  },
  bold: {
    fontWeight: "bold"
  }
});

export default styles;
```

Within *index.js*, we can import our styles like so:

```
import styles from "./styles";
```

Then we can use them in our component (Example 5-7).

Example 5-7. Importing styles from an external JavaScript file

```
import React, { Component } from "react";
import { StyleSheet, View, Text } from "react-native";
import styles from "./styles";

class ComponentName extends Component {
  render() {
    return (
      <Text style={[styles.text, styles.bold]}>
        Hello, world
      </Text>
    );
  }
}
```

Passing Styles as Props

Styles may also be passed as properties on a component.

You can use this pattern to create extensible components, which can be more effectively controlled and styled by their parents. For example, a component might take in an optional style prop (Example 5-8). This is a good way to mimic the "cascading" behavior of CSS.

Example 5-8. Components can receive style objects via props

```
import React, { Component } from "react";
import { View, Text } from "react-native";

class CustomizableText extends Component {
  render() {
    return (
      <Text style={[{fontSize: 18}, this.props.style]}>
        Hello, world
      </Text>
    );
  }
}
```

By adding `this.props.style` to the end of the styles array, we ensure that you can override the default props.

Reusing and Sharing Styles

We typically prefer to reuse styled components rather than reusing styles, but there are clearly some instances in which you will want to share styles between components. In this case, a common pattern is to organize your project roughly like so:

```
- js
  |- components
    |- Button
      |- index.js
      |- styles.js
  |- styles
    |- styles.js
    |- colors.js
    |- fonts.js
```

By having separate directories for components and for styles, you can keep the intended use of each file clear based on context. A component's folder should contain its React class, as well as any component-specific files. Shared styles should be kept out of component folders. Shared styles may include things such as your palette, fonts, standardized margins and padding, and so on.

styles/styles.js imports the other shared styles files and exposes them; then your components can import *styles.js* and use shared files as needed. Or you may prefer to have components import specific stylesheets from the *styles/* directory instead.

Because we've now moved our styles into JavaScript, organizing them is really a question of general code organization—there's no single correct approach here.

Positioning and Designing Layouts

One of the biggest changes when working with styling in React Native is positioning. CSS supports a proliferation of positioning techniques. Between float, absolute positioning, tables, block layout, and more, it's easy to get lost! React Native's approach to positioning is more focused, relying primarily on flexbox as well as absolute positioning, along with the familiar properties of margin and padding. In this section, we'll look at how layouts are constructed in React Native, and finish off by building a layout in the style of a Mondrian painting.

Using Layouts with Flexbox

Flexbox is a CSS3 layout mode. Unlike existing layout modes such as block and inline, flexbox gives us a direction-agnostic way of constructing layouts. (That's right: finally, vertically centering is easy!) React Native leans heavily on flexbox. If you want to read more about the general specification, the MDN documentation (*http://mzl.la/1Ta8Zcj*) is a good place to start.

With React Native, the following flexbox props are available:

- flex
- flexDirection
- flexWrap
- alignSelf
- alignItems

Additionally, these related values impact layout:

- height
- width
- margin
- border
- padding

If you have worked with flexbox on the web before, there won't be many surprises here. Because flexbox is so important to constructing layouts in React Native, though, we'll spend some time now exploring how it works.

The basic idea behind flexbox is that you should be able to create predictably structured layouts, even with dynamically sized elements. Because we're designing for mobile and need to accommodate multiple screen sizes and orientations, this is a useful (dare I say necessary?) feature.

We'll start with a parent `<View>` and some children:

```
<View style={styles.parent}>
  <Text style={styles.child}> Child One </Text>
  <Text style={styles.child}> Child Two </Text>
  <Text style={styles.child}> Child Three </Text>
</View>
```

We've applied some basic styles to the views, but haven't touched the positioning yet:

```
const styles = StyleSheet.create({
  parent: {
    backgroundColor: '#F5FCFF',
    borderColor: '#0099AA',
    borderWidth: 5,
    marginTop: 30
  },
  child: {
    borderColor: '#AA0099',
    borderWidth: 2,
    textAlign: 'center',
    fontSize: 24,
  }
});
```

The resulting layout is shown in Figure 5-1.

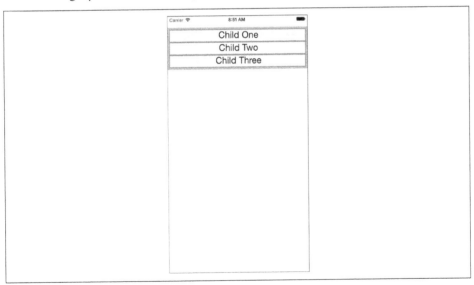

Figure 5-1. The layout before we add flex properties

Next, we will set `flex` on both the parent and the child. By setting the `flex` property, we are explicitly opting in to flexbox behavior. `flex` takes a number, which determines the relative weight each child gets; by setting it to 1, we weight each child equally.

We also set `flexDirection: 'column'` so that the children are laid out vertically. If we switch this to `flexDirection: 'row'`, the children will be laid out horizontally instead. These changes to the styles can be seen in Example 5-9. Figure 5-2 illustrates the difference in how these values impact the layout.

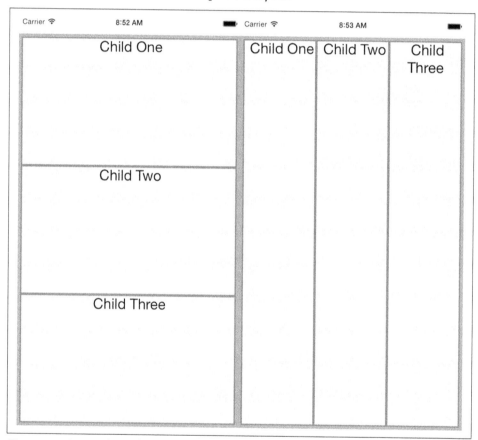

Figure 5-2. Setting basic flex properties and flexDirection; setting flexDirection to column (left) and setting flexDirection to row (right)

Example 5-9. Changing the flex and flexDirection properties

```
const styles = StyleSheet.create({
  parent: {
    flex: 1,
```

```
      flexDirection: 'column',
      backgroundColor: '#F5FCFF',
      borderColor: '#0099AA',
      borderWidth: 5,
      marginTop: 30
    },
    child: {
      flex: 1,
      borderColor: '#AA0099',
      borderWidth: 2,
      textAlign: 'center',
      fontSize: 24,
    }
});
```

If we set `alignItems`, the children will no longer expand to fill all available space in both directions. Because we have set `flexDirection: 'row'`, they will expand to fill the row. However, now they will take only up as much vertical space as they need.

Then, the `alignItems` value determines *where* they are positioned along the cross-axis. The cross-axis is the axis orthogonal to the `flexDirection`. In this case, the cross-axis is vertical. `flex-start` places the children at the top, `center` centers them, and `flex-end` places them at the bottom.

Let's see what happens when we set `alignItems` (the result is shown in Figure 5-3):

```
const styles = StyleSheet.create({
  parent: {
    flex: 1,
    flexDirection: "row",
    alignItems: "flex-start",
    backgroundColor: "#F5FCFF",
    borderColor: "#0099AA",
    borderWidth: 5,
    marginTop: 30
  },
  child: {
    flex: 1,
    borderColor: "#AA0099",
    borderWidth: 2,
    textAlign: "center",
    fontSize: 24,
  }
});
```

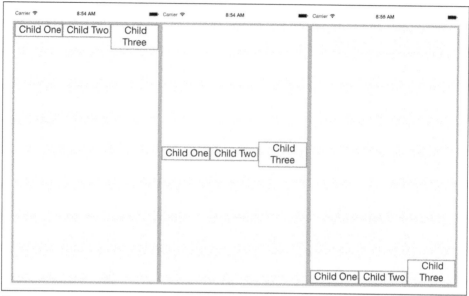

Figure 5-3. Setting alignItems positions children on the cross-axis, which is the axis orthogonal to the flexDirection; here, we see flex-start, center, and flex-end

Using Absolute Positioning

In addition to flexbox, React Native supports absolute positioning. It works much as it does on the web. You can enable it by setting the `position` property:

```
position: absolute
```

Then you can control the component's positioning with the familiar properties `left`, `right`, `top`, and `bottom`.

An absolutely positioned child will apply these coordinates relative to its parent's position, so you can lay out a parent element using flexbox and then use absolute position for a child within it.

There are some limitations to this. We don't have `z-index`, for instance, so layering views on top of each other is a bit complicated. The last view in a stack typically takes precedence.

Absolute positioning can be very useful. For instance, if you want to create a container view that sits below the phone's status bar, absolute positioning makes this easy:

```
container: {
  position: "absolute",
  top: 30,
  left: 0,
```

```
    right: 0,
    bottom: 0
}
```

Putting It Together

Let's try using these positioning techniques to create a more complicated layout. Say we want to mimic a Mondrian painting. Figure 5-4 shows the end result.

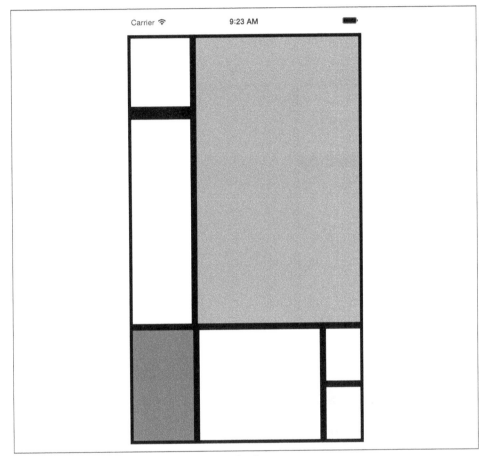

Figure 5-4. We'll use flexbox to construct this layout

How should we go about constructing this kind of layout?

To start with, we create a `parent` style to act as the container. We will use absolute positioning on the parent because it's most appropriate: we want it to fill all available space except for a 30-pixel offset at the top to accommodate the status bar at the top of the screen. We'll also set its `flexDirection` to `column`:

```
parent: {
  flexDirection: "column",
  position: "absolute",
  top: 30,
  left: 0,
  right: 0,
  bottom: 0
}
```

Looking back at the image, we can divide the layout into larger blocks. These divisions are in many ways arbitrary, so we'll pick an option and roll with it. Figure 5-5 shows one way we can segment the layout.

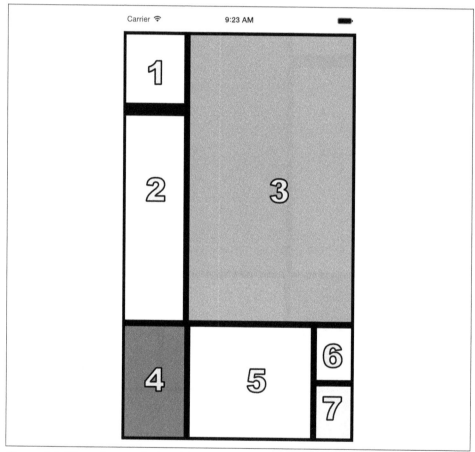

Figure 5-5. The order in which we'll style the sections

We start by cutting the layout into a top and bottom block:

```
<View style={styles.parent}>
  <View style={styles.topBlock}>
```

```
      </View>
      <View style={styles.bottomBlock}>
      </View>
    </View>
```

Then we add in the next layer. This includes both a "left column" and "bottom right" sector, as well as the actual <View> components for cells three, four, and five:

```
  <View style={styles.parent}>
    <View style={styles.topBlock}>
      <View style={styles.leftCol}>
      </View>
      <View style={[styles.cellThree, styles.base]} />
    </View>
    <View style={styles.bottomBlock}>
      <View style={[styles.cellFour, styles.base]}/>
      <View style={[styles.cellFive, styles.base]}/>
      <View style={styles.bottomRight}>
      </View>
    </View>
  </View>
```

The final markup contains all seven cells. Example 5-10 shows the full component.

Example 5-10. styles/Mondrian/index.js

```
import React, { Component } from "react";
import { StyleSheet, Text, View } from "react-native";

import styles from "./style";

class Mondrian extends Component {
  render() {
    return (
      <View style={styles.parent}>
        <View style={styles.topBlock}>
          <View style={styles.leftCol}>
            <View style={[styles.cellOne, styles.base]} />
            <View style={[styles.base, styles.cellTwo]} />
          </View>
          <View style={[styles.cellThree, styles.base]} />
        </View>
        <View style={styles.bottomBlock}>
          <View style={[styles.cellFour, styles.base]} />
          <View style={[styles.cellFive, styles.base]} />
          <View style={styles.bottomRight}>
            <View style={[styles.cellSix, styles.base]} />
            <View style={[styles.cellSeven, styles.base]} />
          </View>
        </View>
      </View>
    );
```

```
    }
  }
}

export default Mondrian;
```

Now let's add the styles that make it work (Example 5-11).

Example 5-11. styles/Mondrian/style.js

```
import React from "react";
import { StyleSheet } from "react-native";

const styles = StyleSheet.create({
  parent: {
    flexDirection: "column",
    position: "absolute",
    top: 30,
    left: 0,
    right: 0,
    bottom: 0
  },
  base: { borderColor: "#000000", borderWidth: 5 },
  topBlock: { flexDirection: "row", flex: 5 },
  leftCol: { flex: 2 },
  bottomBlock: { flex: 2, flexDirection: "row" },
  bottomRight: { flexDirection: "column", flex: 2 },
  cellOne: { flex: 1, borderBottomWidth: 15 },
  cellTwo: { flex: 3 },
  cellThree: { backgroundColor: "#FF0000", flex: 5 },
  cellFour: { flex: 3, backgroundColor: "#0000FF" },
  cellFive: { flex: 6 },
  cellSix: { flex: 1 },
  cellSeven: { flex: 1, backgroundColor: "#FFFF00" }
});

export default styles;
```

Summary

In this chapter, we looked at how styles work in React Native. While in many ways styling is similar to how CSS works on the web, React Native introduces a different structure and approach to styling. There's plenty of new material to digest here! At this point, you should be able to use styles effectively to create the mobile UIs you need with React Native. And best of all, experimenting with styles is easy: being able to hit "reload" in the simulator grants us a tight feedback loop. (It's worth noting that with traditional mobile development, editing a style would typically require rebuilding your application. Yikes.)

If you want more practice with styles, try going back to the *New York Times* Best Sellers list or weather applications and adjusting their styling and layouts. As we build more sample applications in future chapters, you'll have plenty of material to practice with, too!

Platform APIs

When building mobile applications, you will naturally want to take advantage of the host platform's specific APIs. React Native makes it easy to access things like the phone's camera roll, location, and persistent storage. These platform APIs are made available to React Native through included modules, which provide us with easy-to-use asynchronous JavaScript interfaces to these capabilities.

React Native does not wrap all of its host platform's functionality by default; some platform APIs will require you to either write your own modules, or use modules written by others in the React Native community. We will cover that process in Chapter 7. The docs (*https://facebook.github.io/react-native*) are the best place to check if an API is supported.

This chapter covers some of the available platform APIs. For our example, we'll make some modifications to the weather application from earlier. We'll add geolocation to the app so that it detects the user's location automatically. We will also add "memory" to the app so it will remember your previously searched locations. Finally, we'll use the camera roll to change the background image to one of the user's photos.

While relevant code snippets will be presented in each section, the full code for the application is included in "The SmarterWeather Application" on page 104.

Using Geolocation

For mobile applications, knowing the user's location is often critical. It allows you to serve the user contextually relevant information. Many mobile applications make extensive use of this data.

React Native has built-in support for geolocation. This is provided as a platform-agnostic "polyfill." It returns data based on the MDN Geolocation API web specification (*http://mzl.la/1lELM6N*). Because we're using the Geolocation specification, you won't need to deal with platform-specific APIs like Location Services, and any location-aware code you write should be fully portable.

Reading the User's Location

Using the Geolocation API to get a user's location is a breeze. As shown in Example 6-1, we need to make a call to `navigator.geolocation`.

Example 6-1. Getting the user's location with a navigator.geolocation call

```
navigator.geolocation.getCurrentPosition(
  (position) => {
    console.log(position);
  },
  (error) => {alert(error.message)},
  {enableHighAccuracy: true, timeout: 20000, maximumAge: 1000}
);
```

The position will be printed to the JavaScript console; see "Debugging with console.log" on page 141 for more information on how to work with the console.

In conformance to the Geolocation specification, we don't import the location API as a separate module; it's simply available for our use.

The `getCurrentPosition` call takes three arguments: a success callback, an error callback, and a set of `geoOptions`. Only the success callback is required.

The `position` object passed to the success callback will contain coordinates, as well as a timestamp. Example 6-2 shows the format and possible values.

Example 6-2. Shape of the response returned from a getCurrentPosition call

```
{
  coords: {
    speed:-1,
    longitude:-122.03031802,
    latitude:37.33259551999998,
    accuracy:500,
    heading:-1,
    altitude:0,
    altitudeAccuracy:-1
  },
  timestamp:459780747046.605
}
```

`geoOptions` should be an object, which optionally includes the keys `timeout`, `enable HighAccuracy`, and `maximumAge`. `timeout` is probably the most relevant of the bunch when it comes to affecting your application logic.

Note that this won't actually work until you add the proper permissions to either your *Info.plist* file (for iOS) or your *AndroidManifest.xml* file (for Android), as we'll discuss next.

Handling Permissions

Location data is sensitive information, and therefore will not be accessible to your application by default. Your application should be able to handle permissions being accepted or rejected.

Most mobile platforms have some notion of location permissions. A user may opt to block Location Services entirely on iOS, for instance, or they may manage permissions on a per-app basis. It's important to note that location permissions can be revoked at essentially any point in time. Your application should always be prepared for a geolocation call to fail.

In order to access location data, first you need to declare that your application intends to use location data.

On iOS, you'll need to include the key `NSLocationWhenInUseUsageDescription` in your *Info.plist* file. This should be included by default when you create a new React Native application.

On Android, you'll need to add the following to your *AndroidManifest.xml* file:

```
<uses-permission android:name="android.permission.ACCESS_FINE_LOCATION" />
```

The first time your application attempts to access the user's location, the user will be presented with a permissions dialog like the one shown in Figure 6-1.

Figure 6-1. Location request

While this dialog is active, neither callback will fire; once the user selects an option, the appropriate callback will be invoked. This setting will persist for your application, so the next time such a check won't be necessary.

If the user denies permissions, you can fail silently if you want, but most apps use an alert dialog to request permissions again.

Testing Geolocation in Emulated Devices

Chances are, you'll be doing most of your testing and development from within a simulator, or at the very least, at your desk. How can you test how your app will behave at different locations?

The iOS simulator allows you to easily spoof a different location. By default, you'll be placed near Apple HQ in California, but you can specify any other coordinates as well by navigating to Debug → Location → Custom Location..., as shown in Figure 6-2.

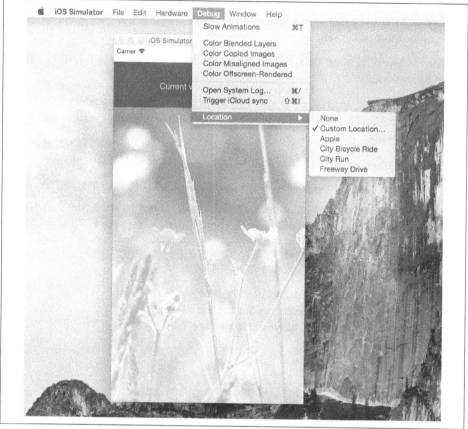

Figure 6-2. Picking a location from the iOS simulator

Similarly, on Android, you can select which GPS coordinates to send (Figure 6-3). You can even import data and control the playback speed to simulate changing locations.

Figure 6-3. Picking a location from the Android emulator

It's good practice to try out different locations as part of your testing process. For rigorous testing, of course, you will want to load your application onto an actual device.

Watching the User's Location

You can also set a watch on the user's location, and receive updates whenever it changes. This can be used to track a user's location over time, or just to ensure that your app receives the most up-to-date position:

```
this.watchID = navigator.geolocation.watchPosition((position) => {
  this.setState({position: position});
});
```

Note that you'll want to clear the watch when your component unmounts as well:

```
componentWillUnmount() {
  navigator.geolocation.clearWatch(this.watchID);
}
```

Working Around Limitations

Because geolocation is based on the MDN specification, it leaves out more advanced location-based features. For example, iOS provides a Geofencing API, which allows your application to receive notifications when the user enters or leaves a designated geographical region (the *geofence*). React Native does not expose this API.

This means that if you want to use location-based features that aren't included in the Geolocation MDN specification, you'll need to port them yourself.

Updating the Weather Application

The SmarterWeather application is an updated version of the weather application, which now makes use of the Geolocation API. You can see these changes in Figure 6-4.

Most notable is a new component, <LocationButton>, which fetches the user's current location and invokes a callback when pressed. The code for the <Location Button> is shown in Example 6-3.

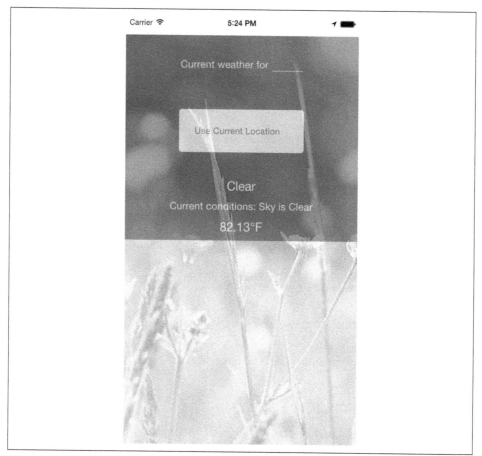

Figure 6-4. Displaying forecast based on the user's current location

Example 6-3. smarter-weather/LocationButton/index.js: when pressed, the button gets the user's location

```
import React, { Component } from "react";

import Button from "./../Button";
import styles from "./style.js";

const style = { backgroundColor: "#DDDDDD" };

class LocationButton extends Component {
  _onPress() {
    navigator.geolocation.getCurrentPosition(
      initialPosition => {
        this.props.onGetCoords(
          initialPosition.coords.latitude,
          initialPosition.coords.longitude
        );
      },
      error => {
        alert(error.message);
      },
      { enableHighAccuracy: true, timeout: 20000, maximumAge: 1000 }
    );
  }

  render() {
    return (
      <Button
        label="Use Current Location"
        style={style}
        onPress={this._onPress.bind(this)}
      />
    );
  }
}

export default LocationButton;
```

The `<Button>` component used by `<LocationButton>` is included at the end of this chapter; it simply wraps a `<Text>` component in an appropriate `<TouchableHighlight>` with some basic styling.

We've also had to update the main *weather_project.js* file to accommodate two kinds of queries (Example 6-4). Happily, the OpenWeatherMap API allows us to query by latitude and longitude as well as zip code.

Example 6-4. Adding _getForecastForCoords and _getForecastForZip functions

```
const WEATHER_API_KEY = 'bbeb34ebf60ad50f7893e7440a1e2b0b';
const API_STEM = 'http://api.openweathermap.org/data/2.5/weather?';

...

_getForecastForZip: function(zip) {
  this._getForecast(
    `${API_STEM}q=${zip}&units=imperial&APPID=${WEATHER_API_KEY}`);
},

_getForecastForCoords: function(lat, lon) {
  this._getForecast(
    `${API_STEM}lat=${lat}&lon=${lon}&units=imperial&APPID=${WEATHER_API_KEY}`);
},

_getForecast: function(url, cb) {
  fetch(url)
    .then((response) => response.json())
    .then((responseJSON) => {
      console.log(responseJSON);
      this.setState({
        forecast: {
          main: responseJSON.weather[0].main,
          description: responseJSON.weather[0].description,
          temp: responseJSON.main.temp
        }
      });
    })
    .catch((error) => {
      console.warn(error);
    });
}
```

Then we include the <LocationButton> in the main view with _getForecastFor
Coords as the callback:

```
<LocationButton onGetCoords={this._getForecastForCoords}/>
```

Relevant style updates are not shown here, as the fully updated application code will
be included at the end of this chapter.

There's plenty of work left to be done if you wanted to actually ship this to users—for
example, a more complete app would include better error messages and additional UI
feedback. But basic location fetching is surprisingly straightforward!

Accessing the User's Images and Camera

Project with Native Code Required

The examples in this section apply only to projects created with react-native-init, or ejected projects created with create-react-native-app. For more information, see Appendix C.

Having access to a phone's local images and camera is another critical part of many mobile applications. In this section, we'll explore your options for interacting with users' image data as well as the camera.

We'll still be using the SmarterWeather project. Let's change the background to use an image from the user's photos.

Interacting with the CameraRoll Module

React Native provides an interface into the camera roll, which contains the images stored on the user's phone that were taken with the camera.

Interacting with the camera roll in its most basic form is not too complicated. First we import the `CameraRoll` module, as per usual:

```
import { CameraRoll } from "react-native";
```

Then, we make use of the module to fetch information about the user's photos, as shown in Example 6-5.

Example 6-5. Basic usage of CameraRoll.getPhotos

```
CameraRoll.getPhotos(
  {first: 1},
  (data) => {
    console.log(data);
  },
  (error) => {
    console.warn(error);
  });
```

We make a call to `getPhotos` with the appropriate query, and it returns some data related to the camera roll images.

In `SmarterWeather`, let's replace the top-level `<Image>` component with a new component, `<PhotoBackdrop>` (Example 6-6). For now, `<PhotoBackdrop>` simply displays a photo from the user's camera roll.

Example 6-6. smarter-weather/PhotoBackdrop/index.js

```
import React, { Component } from "react";

import { Image, CameraRoll } from "react-native";

import styles from "./style";

class PhotoBackdrop extends Component {
  constructor(props) {
    super(props);
    this.state = { photoSource: null };
  }

  componentDidMount() {
    CameraRoll.getPhotos({ first: 1 }).then(data => {
      this.setState({ photoSource: { uri: data.edges[3].node.image.uri } });
    }, error => {
      console.warn(error);
    });
  }

  render() {
    return (
      <Image
        style={styles.backdrop}
        source={this.state.photoSource}
        resizeMode="cover"
      >
        {this.props.children}
      </Image>
    );
  }
}

export default PhotoBackdrop;
```

`CameraRoll.getPhotos` takes three arguments: an object with params, a success callback, and an error callback.

Requesting Images with GetPhotoParams

The `getPhotoParams` object can take a variety of options. We can take a look at the React Native source code (*http://bit.ly/1kPZnrQ*) to see which options are available to us:

first

    Number; the number of photos wanted in reverse order of the photo application (i.e., most recent first for `SavedPhotos`).

after
> String; a cursor that matches `page_info {end_cursor}` returned from a previous call to `getPhotos`.

groupTypes
> String; specifies which group to use to filter results. May be `Album`, `All`, `Event`, and so on; the full list of `GroupTypes` is specified in the source.

groupName
> String; specifies a filter on group names, such as `Recent Photos` or an album title.

assetType
> One of `All`, `Photos`, or `Videos`; specifies a filter on asset type.

mimeTypes
> Array of strings; filters based on mimetype (such as *image/jpeg*).

In our basic invocation of `getPhotos` in Example 6-5, our `getPhotoParams` object was quite simple:

```
{first: 1}
```

This means, simply, that we are looking for the most recent photo.

Rendering an Image from the Camera Roll

How do we render an image we've received from the camera roll? Let's take a look at that success callback:

```
(data) => {
  this.setState({
    photoSource: {uri: data.edges[0].node.image.uri}
  })},
```

The structure of the data object is not immediately apparent, so you'll likely want to use the debugger to inspect the object. Each of the objects in `data.edges` has a `node` that represents a photo; from there, you can get the URI of the actual asset.

You may recall that an `<Image>` component can take a URI as its `source` property. So, we can render an image obtained from the camera roll by setting the source property appropriately:

```
<Image source={this.state.photoSource} />
```

That's it! You can see the resulting application, including the image, in Figure 6-5.

Figure 6-5. Rendering an image from the camera roll

Uploading an Image to a Server

What if you want to upload a photo somewhere? React Native ships with built-in image uploading functionality in the XHR module. The basic approach looks like this:

```
let formdata = new FormData();
...
formdata.append('image', {...this.state.randomPhoto, name: 'image.jpg'});
...
xhr.send(formdata);
```

XHR is short for `XMLHttpRequest`. React Native implements the XHR API on top of the iOS networking APIs. Similar to geolocation, React Native's XHR implementation is based on the MDN specification (*http://bit.ly/xmlhttpreq*).

Using XHR for network requests is somewhat more complex than the Fetch API, but the basic approach should look something like Example 6-7.

Example 6-7. Basic structure for POSTing a photo using XHR

```
let xhr = new XMLHttpRequest();
xhr.open('POST', 'http://posttestserver.com/post.php');
let formdata = new FormData();
formdata.append('image', {...this.state.photo, name: 'image.jpg'});
xhr.send(formdata);
```

Omitted here are the various callbacks you will want to register with the XHR request.

Storing Persistent Data with AsyncStorage

Most applications will need to keep track of some variety of data persistently. How do you accomplish this with React Native?

React Native provides us with AsyncStorage, a key-value store that is global to your application. If you have used LocalStorage on the web, AsyncStorage ought to feel quite similar. Its implementation varies by platform, but the JavaScript API is the same regardless of whether you are using Android or iOS.

Let's take a look at how to use the React Native AsyncStorage module.

The storage key used by AsyncStorage can be any string; it's customary to use the format @AppName:key, like so:

```
const STORAGE_KEY = '@SmarterWeather:zip';
```

The AsyncStorage module returns a promise in response to both getItem and setItem. For the SmarterWeather app, let's load the stored zip code in componentDidMount:

```
AsyncStorage.getItem(STORAGE_KEY)
  .then((value) => {
    if (value !== null) {
      this._getForecastForZip(value);
    }
  })
  .catch((error) => console.log('AsyncStorage error: ' + error.message))
  .done();
```

Then, in _getForecaseForZip, we can store the zip code value:

```
AsyncStorage.setItem(STORAGE_KEY, zip)
  .then(() => console.log('Saved selection to disk: ' + zip))
  .catch((error) => console.log('AsyncStorage error: ' + error.message))
  .done();
```

AsyncStorage also provides methods for deleting keys, merging keys, and fetching all available keys.

The SmarterWeather Application

All of the example code in this chapter can be found in the *SmarterWeather/* directory. The original weather application from Chapter 3 has changed quite a bit, so let's take a look at the structure of the entire application again (Example 6-8).

Example 6-8. Contents of the SmarterWeather project

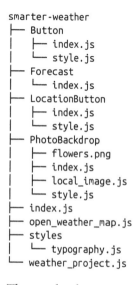

```
smarter-weather
├── Button
│   ├── index.js
│   └── style.js
├── Forecast
│   └── index.js
├── LocationButton
│   ├── index.js
│   └── style.js
├── PhotoBackdrop
│   ├── flowers.png
│   ├── index.js
│   ├── local_image.js
│   └── style.js
├── index.js
├── open_weather_map.js
├── styles
│   └── typography.js
└── weather_project.js
```

The top-level component is located in *weather_project.js*. Shared font styles are located in *styles/typography.js*. The folders *Forecast/*, *PhotoBackdrop/*, *Button/*, and *LocationButton/* all contain React components used in the new SmarterWeather application.

The <WeatherProject> Component

The top-level <WeatherProject> component is located in *weather_project.js* (Example 6-9). This includes the use of AsyncStorage to store the most recent location.

Example 6-9. smarter-weather/weather_project.js

```
import React, { Component } from "react";
import {
  StyleSheet,
```

```
  Text,
  View,
  TextInput,
  AsyncStorage,
  Image
} from "react-native";

import Forecast from "./Forecast";
import LocationButton from "./LocationButton";
import textStyles from "./styles/typography.js";

const STORAGE_KEY = "@SmarterWeather:zip";

import OpenWeatherMap from "./open_weather_map";

// This version uses flowers.png from local assets
import PhotoBackdrop from "./PhotoBackdrop/local_image";

// This version pulls a specified photo from the camera roll
// import PhotoBackdrop from './PhotoBackdrop';

class WeatherProject extends Component {
  constructor(props) {
    super(props);
    this.state = { forecast: null };
  }

  componentDidMount() {
    AsyncStorage
      .getItem(STORAGE_KEY)
      .then(value => {
        if (value !== null) {
          this._getForecastForZip(value);
        }
      })
      .catch(error => console.error("AsyncStorage error: " + error.message))
      .done();
  }

  _getForecastForZip = zip => {
    // Store zip code
    AsyncStorage
      .setItem(STORAGE_KEY, zip)
      .then(() => console.log("Saved selection to disk: " + zip))
      .catch(error => console.error("AsyncStorage error: " + error.message))
      .done();

    OpenWeatherMap.fetchZipForecast(zip).then(forecast => {
      this.setState({ forecast: forecast });
    });
  };
```

```
_getForecastForCoords = (lat, lon) => {
  OpenWeatherMap.fetchLatLonForecast(lat, lon).then(forecast => {
    this.setState({ forecast: forecast });
  });
};

_handleTextChange = event => {
  let zip = event.nativeEvent.text;
  this._getForecastForZip(zip);
};

render() {
  let content = null;
  if (this.state.forecast !== null) {
    content = (
      <View style={styles.row}>
        <Forecast
          main={this.state.forecast.main}
          temp={this.state.forecast.temp}
        />
      </View>
    );
  }

  return (
    <PhotoBackdrop>
      <View style={styles.overlay}>
        <View style={styles.row}>
          <Text style={textStyles.mainText}>
            Forecast for
          </Text>

          <View style={styles.zipContainer}>
            <TextInput
              style={[textStyles.mainText, styles.zipCode]}
              onSubmitEditing={this._handleTextChange}
              underlineColorAndroid="transparent"
            />
          </View>
        </View>

        <View style={styles.row}>
          <LocationButton onGetCoords={this._getForecastForCoords} />
        </View>

        {content}

      </View>
    </PhotoBackdrop>
  );
}
}
```

```
const styles = StyleSheet.create({
  overlay: { backgroundColor: "rgba(0,0,0,0.1)" },
  row: {
    flexDirection: "row",
    flexWrap: "nowrap",
    alignItems: "center",
    justifyContent: "center",
    padding: 24
  },
  zipContainer: {
    borderBottomColor: "#DDDDDD",
    borderBottomWidth: 1,
    marginLeft: 5,
    marginTop: 3,
    width: 80,
    height: textStyles.baseFontSize * 2,
    justifyContent: "flex-end"
  },
  zipCode: { flex: 1 }
});

export default WeatherProject;
```

It makes use of shared styles located in *styles/typography.js* (Example 6-10).

Example 6-10. Shared font styles are located in smarter-weather/styles/typography.js

```
import { StyleSheet } from "react-native";

const baseFontSize = 24;

const styles = StyleSheet.create({
  bigText: { fontSize: baseFontSize + 8, color: "#FFFFFF" },
  mainText: { fontSize: baseFontSize, color: "#FFFFFF" }
});

// For use elsewhere...
styles["baseFontSize"] = baseFontSize;

export default styles;
```

The <Forecast> Component

The <Forecast> component displays the forecast information, including the temperature. It's used by the <WeatherProject> component just shown. The code for the <Forecast> component is provided in Example 6-11.

Example 6-11. <Forecast> component renders information about the forecast

```javascript
import React, { Component } from "react";

import { Text, View, StyleSheet } from "react-native";

class Forecast extends Component {
  render() {
    return (
      <View style={styles.forecast}>
        <Text style=>
          {this.props.temp}°F
        </Text>
        <Text style=>
          {this.props.main}
        </Text>
      </View>
    );
  }
}

const styles = StyleSheet.create({ forecast: { alignItems: "center" } });

export default Forecast;
```

The <Button> Component

The <Button> component is a reusable container-style component. It provides a properly styled <Text> wrapped by a <TouchableHighlight>. The main component file is provided in Example 6-12, and its associated styles are provided in Example 6-13.

Example 6-12. The <Button> component provides an appropriately styled <TouchableHighlight> containing a <Text>

```javascript
import React, { Component } from "react";

import { Text, View, TouchableHighlight } from "react-native";

import styles from "./style";

class Button extends Component {
  render() {
    return (
      <TouchableHighlight onPress={this.props.onPress}>
        <View style={[styles.button, this.props.style]}>
          <Text>
            {this.props.label}
          </Text>
        </View>
```

```
        </TouchableHighlight>
    );
  }
}

export default Button;
```

Example 6-13. Styles for the <Button> component

```
import { StyleSheet } from "react-native";

const styles = StyleSheet.create({
  button: { backgroundColor: "#FFDDFF", padding: 25, borderRadius: 5 }
});

export default styles;
```

The <LocationButton> Component

When pressed, the <LocationButton> fetches the user's location and invokes a call-back. The component's main JavaScript file is provided in Example 6-14, and its styles are provided in Example 6-15.

Example 6-14. The <LocationButton> component

```
import React, { Component } from "react";

import Button from "././../Button";
import styles from "./style.js";

const style = { backgroundColor: "#DDDDDD" };

class LocationButton extends Component {
  _onPress() {
    navigator.geolocation.getCurrentPosition(
      initialPosition => {
        this.props.onGetCoords(
          initialPosition.coords.latitude,
          initialPosition.coords.longitude
        );
      },
      error => {
        alert(error.message);
      },
      { enableHighAccuracy: true, timeout: 20000, maximumAge: 1000 }
    );
  }

  render() {
    return (
```

```
      <Button
        label="Use Current Location"
        style={style}
        onPress={this._onPress.bind(this)}
      />
    );
  }
}

export default LocationButton;
```

Example 6-15. Styles for <LocationButton>

```
import { StyleSheet } from "react-native";

const styles = StyleSheet.create({
  locationButton: { width: 200, padding: 25, borderRadius: 5 }
});

export default styles;
```

The <PhotoBackdrop> Component

There are two versions of <PhotoBackdrop> provided, to demonstrate different meth‐
ods of selecting an image for the background. The first, provided in Example 6-16
and listed as *local_image.js* in the GitHub repository, uses a simple require call to load
a standard image asset. The second, as seen in Example 6-17, selects an image from
the user's camera roll.

Example 6-16. local_image.js is the original version; it uses a simple require call

```
import React, { Component } from "react";

import { Image } from "react-native";

import styles from "./style.js";

class PhotoBackdrop extends Component {
  render() {
    return (
      <Image
        style={styles.backdrop}
        source={require("./flowers.png")}
        resizeMode="cover"
      >
        {this.props.children}
      </Image>
    );
  }
}
```

```
export default PhotoBackdrop;
```

Example 6-17. src/smarter-weather/PhotoBackdrop/index.js programmatically selects an image from the camera roll

```
import React, { Component } from "react";

import { Image, CameraRoll } from "react-native";

import styles from "./style";

class PhotoBackdrop extends Component {
  constructor(props) {
    super(props);
    this.state = { photoSource: null };
  }

  componentDidMount() {
    CameraRoll.getPhotos({ first: 1 }).then(data => {
      this.setState({ photoSource: { uri: data.edges[3].node.image.uri } });
    }, error => {
      console.warn(error);
    });
  }

  render() {
    return (
      <Image
        style={styles.backdrop}
        source={this.state.photoSource}
        resizeMode="cover"
      >
        {this.props.children}
      </Image>
    );
  }
}

export default PhotoBackdrop;
```

Both versions share the same stylesheet, shown in Example 6-18.

Example 6-18. Both versions of the <PhotoBackdrop> use this stylesheet

```
import { StyleSheet } from "react-native";

export default StyleSheet.create({
  backdrop: {
    flex: 1,
    flexDirection: "column",
```

```
    width: undefined,
    height: undefined
  },
  button: { flex: 1, margin: 100, alignItems: "center" }
});
```

Summary

In this chapter, we made some modifications to the weather application. We looked at the Geolocation, CameraRoll, and AsyncStorage APIs, and learned how to incorporate these modules into our applications.

When React Native ships with support for a host platform API, it makes usage a breeze. But what happens if React Native does not yet support a given API, such as in the case of video playback, and you want to use a library or module that isn't yet available in JavaScript? In the next chapter, we'll take a closer look at this scenario.

Modules and Native Code

Project with Native Code Required

The examples in this section apply only to projects created with react-native-init and ejected projects created with create-react-native-app. For more information, see Appendix C.

In Chapter 6, we looked at some of the APIs that React Native exposes for interacting with the host platform. Because support for those APIs is built into React Native, they're quite easy to use. What happens when we want to use an API that isn't supported by React Native?

In this chapter, we'll look at how to install modules written by members of the React Native community using npm. We'll also take a closer look at one such module, react-native-video, and learn how the RCTBridgeModule can allow you to add JavaScript interfaces to existing Objective-C APIs. We'll also look at importing pure JavaScript libraries into your project, and how to manage dependencies.

Though we will be looking at some Objective-C and Java code this chapter, don't be alarmed! We'll be taking it slowly. A full introduction to mobile development for iOS and Android is beyond the scope of this book, but we'll walk through some examples together.

Installing JavaScript Libraries with npm

Before we discuss how native modules work, first we should cover how to install external dependencies in general. React Native uses npm to manage dependencies. npm is the package manager for Node.js, but the npm registry includes packages for all sorts of JavaScript projects, not just Node. npm uses a file called *package.json* to store metadata about your project, including the list of dependencies.

Let's start by creating a fresh project:

```
react-native init Depends
```

After creating a new project, your *package.json* will look something like Example 7-1.

Example 7-1. Depends/package.json

```
{
  "name": "Depends",
  "version": "0.0.1",
  "private": true,
  "scripts": {
    "start": "node node_modules/react-native/local-cli/cli.js start",
    "test": "jest"
  },
  "dependencies": {
    "react": "16.0.0-alpha.12",
    "react-native": "0.45.1"
  },
  "devDependencies": {
    "babel-jest": "20.0.3",
    "babel-preset-react-native": "2.0.0",
    "jest": "20.0.4",
    "react-test-renderer": "16.0.0-alpha.12"
  },
  "jest": {
    "preset": "react-native"
  }
}
```

Note that for now, the only top-level dependencies in your project are `react` and `react-native`. Let's add another dependency!

The lodash library provides a number of helpful utility functions, like a `shuffle` function for arrays. We install it with the `--save` flag to indicate that it should be added to our list of dependencies:

```
npm install --save lodash
```

Now your dependencies in *package.json* should be updated:

```
"dependencies": {
  "lodash": "^4.17.4",
  "react": "16.0.0-alpha.12",
  "react-native": "0.45.1"
}
```

If you want to use lodash in your React Native application, you can now `import` it by name:

```
import _ from "lodash";
```

Let's use lodash to print a random number:

```
import _ from "lodash";
console.warn("Random number: " + _.random(0, 5));
```

It works! But what about other modules? Can you include arbitrary packages by using npm install?

The answer is yes, with some caveats. Any methods that touch the DOM, for instance, will fail. Integrating with existing packages may require some finagling because many packages make assumptions about the environment they'll be running in. But in general, you can take advantage of arbitrary JavaScript packages and use npm to manage your dependencies just like you would on any other JavaScript project.

Installing Third-Party Components with Native Code

Now that we've seen what it's like to add an outside JavaScript library, let's add a React Native component using npm. For this section, we are going to be using react-native-video as our primary example. It's part of the GitHub project react-native-community (*https://github.com/react-native-community*), a collection of high-quality React Native modules.

The react-native-video component is listed in the npm registry (*https://www.npmjs.com/package/react-native-video*). We can add it to our project with npm install:

```
npm install react-native-video --save
```

If we were working with traditional web development, we would be done! react-native-video would now be available to our project. However, this module requires changes to our underlying iOS and Android projects, so there's one more step:

```
react-native link
```

What does react-native link do? It makes modifications to the underlying iOS and Android projects. For iOS, this might entail edits to *AppDelegate.m* and the Xcode project file. For Android, this might include changes to *MainApplication.java*, *settings.gradle*, and *build.gradle*. Typically a module will specify this requirement in its installation instructions.

Note that react-native link will work only with projects generated via react-native init or applications created with create-react-native-app that have since been ejected. Migrating from a create-react-native-app project to a full React Native project is discussed in "Ejecting from Expo" on page 219.

If you are not working with an autogenerated application, you'll need to manually update your project files according to the instructions provided by the module authors.

Now that we have installed the `react-native-video` module, let's test it out. You'll need any MP4 video file for this step. I used a public-domain video from Flickr (*https://www.flickr.com/photos/michal_tuski/27831372885/*).

MP4 assets work just like images in React Native, so you can load the video file like so:

```
let warblerVideo = require("./warbler.mp4");
```

Using the Video Component

We can require the `<Video>` component from our JavaScript code:

```
import Video from "react-native-video"
```

Then use the component just as you normally would. Here, I've set a few of the optional props:

```
<Video source={require("./warbler.mp4")} // Can be a URL or a local file.
       rate={1.0}                        // 0 is paused, 1 is normal.
       volume={1.0}                      // 0 is muted, 1 is normal.
       muted={false}                     // Mutes the audio entirely.
       paused={false}                    // Pauses playback entirely.
       resizeMode="cover"                // Fill the whole screen at aspect ratio.
       repeat={true}                     // Repeat forever.
       style={styles.backgroundVideo} />
```

Ta-da! We have a working video component! It should work on both Android and iOS.

As you can see, including third-party modules with native code is a straightforward process. Many such components are listed in the npm registry and often use the prefix `react-native-`. Take a look around and see what the community has built!

Objective-C Native Modules

Now that we've taken a look at how to install and use a module that includes native code, let's dive into how it works under the hood. We'll start with the Objective-C side of things.

Writing an Objective-C Native Module for iOS

Now that we're using the `react-native-video` module, let's look at how modules like these work under the hood.

The `react-native-video` component is what React refers to as a native module (*http://bit.ly/1PVBCcZ*). The React Native documentation defines a *native module* as "an Objective-C class that implements the RCTBridgeModule protocol." (RCT is an abbreviation for ReaCT.)

Writing Objective-C code is not part of the standard development process with React Native, so don't worry—this is not necessary stuff! But having basic reading knowledge of what's going on will be helpful even if you don't plan on implementing your own native modules (yet).

If you have never worked with Objective-C before, much of the syntax you'll encounter may seem confusing. That's okay! We'll take things slowly. Let's start by building a basic "Hello, World" module.

Objective-C classes usually have a header file that ends in *.h*, which contains the interface for a class. The actual implementation goes in a *.m* file. Let's start by writing our *HelloWorld.h* file, shown in Example 7-2.

Example 7-2. HelloWorld.h

```
#import <React/RCTBridgeModule.h>

@interface HelloWorld : NSObject <RCTBridgeModule>
@end
```

What does this file do? On the first line, we import the `RCTBridgeModule` header. (Note that the # symbol does *not* denote a comment, but rather an `import` statement.) Then on the next line, we declare that the `HelloWorld` class subclasses `NSObject` and implements the `RCTBridgeModule` interface, and end the interface declaration with `@end`.

For historical reasons, many basic types in Objective-C are prefixed with `NS` (`NSString`, `NSObject`, etc.).

Now let's move on to the implementation (Example 7-3).

Example 7-3. HelloWorld.m

```
#import "HelloWorld.h"
#import <React/RCTLog.h>

@implementation HelloWorld

RCT_EXPORT_MODULE();

RCT_EXPORT_METHOD(greeting:(NSString *)name)
{
```

```
    RCTLogInfo(@"Saluton, %@", name);
}

@end
```

In a *.m* file, you'll want to import the corresponding *.h* file, as we do here on the first line. I've also imported *RCTLog.h*, so that we can log things to the console using RCTLogInfo. When importing other classes in Objective-C, you'll almost always want to import the header file, *not* the *.m* file.

The @implementation and @end lines indicate that the contents between them are the implementation of the HelloWorld class.

The remaining lines do the work of making this a React Native module. With RCT_EXPORT_MODULE(), we invoke a special React Native macro that makes this class accessible to the React Native bridge. Similarly, our method definition for greeting:name is prefixed with a macro, RCT_EXPORT_METHOD, which exports the method and thus will expose it to our JavaScript code.

Note that Objective-C methods are named with a somewhat odd syntax. Each parameter's name is included in the method name. It is React Native convention that the JavaScript function name is the Objective-C name up until the first colon, so greeting:name becomes greeting in JavaScript. You may use the macro RCT_REMAP_METHOD to remap this naming if you like.

Now, you might note that these files don't exist in your Xcode project (Figure 7-1).

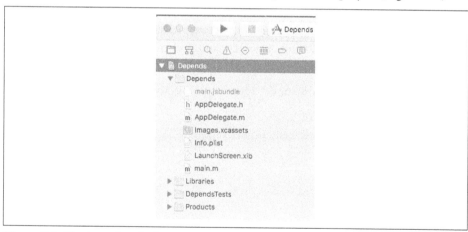

Figure 7-1. Xcode project, before importing our new files

We need to add them to our project in order to include them in our application's build. You can do this by selecting File → Add Files to "Depends" (Figure 7-2).

Figure 7-2. *The Add Files menu option in Xcode*

Select both *HelloWorld.m* and *HelloWorld.h* to add to your project (Figure 7-3).

Figure 7-3. *Importing HelloWorld.m and HelloWorld.h to our project*

Now you should see both files in your Xcode project (Figure 7-4).

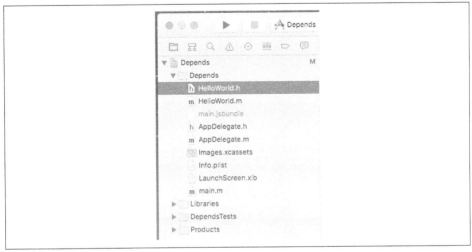

Figure 7-4. *The updated Xcode project's file tree*

Now that our *HelloWorld* files are imported, we can use the `HelloWorld` module from our JavaScript code (Example 7-4).

Example 7-4. Using the HelloWorld module from our JavaScript code

```
import { NativeModules } from "react-native";
NativeModules.HelloWorld.greeting("Bonnie");
```

The output should appear in the console (Figure 7-5), both in Xcode and in the Chrome developer tools, if you choose to enable them.

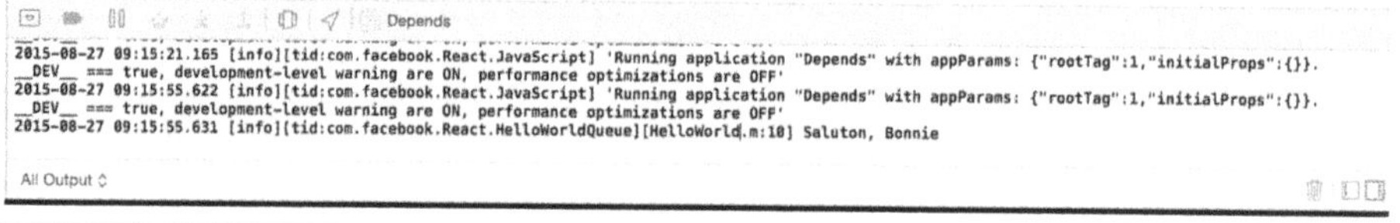

Figure 7-5. Console output, as viewed through the Xcode interface

Note that the syntax for importing native modules is a bit verbose. A common approach is to wrap your native module in a JavaScript module (Example 7-5).

Example 7-5. HelloWorld.js: a JavaScript wrapper for the HelloWorld native module

```
import { NativeModules } from "react-native";
export default NativeModules.HelloWorld;
```

Then, requiring it becomes much more straightforward:

```
import HelloWorld from "./HelloWorld";
```

The *HelloWorld.js* JavaScript file is also a good opportunity to add any JavaScript-side functionality to your module.

Phew. Objective-C can feel verbose, and we have to keep track of a couple of different files. But congratulations: you've written a "Hello, World" for your Objective-C module!

To review, an Objective-C module must do the following in order to be available in React Native:

- Import the `RCTBridgeModule` header
- Declare that your module implements the `RCTBridgeModule` interface
- Call the `RCT_EXPORT_MODULE()` macro
- Have at least one method that is exported using the `RCT_EXPORT_METHOD` macro

Native modules can then make use of any API provided by the iOS SDK. (Note that the API you provide to React Native *must* be asynchronous.) Apple provides extensive documentation for the iOS SDK, and there are many resources available from third parties as well. Note that your developer licenses will come in handy here—it's often difficult to access the SDK documentation without one.

Now that we've written our own basic "Hello, World," let's take a deeper look at how react-native-video is implemented.

Exploring react-native-video for iOS

Just like our HelloWorld module, RCTVideo is a native module, and it implements the RCTBridgeModule protocol. You can see the full code for RCTVideo in the react-native-video GitHub repository (*https://github.com/react-native-community/react-native-video*). We'll be looking at version 1.0.0.

react-native-video is basically a wrapper around the AVPlayer API provided by the iOS SDK. Let's take a closer look at how it works, beginning with the JavaScript entry points *Video.ios.js*.

We can see that it provides a thin wrapper around the native component, RCTVideo, performing some props normalization and a bit of extra rendering logic. The native component is imported at the end:

```
const RCTVideo = requireNativeComponent('RCTVideo', Video, {
  nativeOnly: {
    src: true,
    seek: true,
    fullscreen: true,
  },
});
```

As we saw in our HelloWorld example, that means that somewhere the iOS implementation of the RCTVideo component must be exported from Objective-C. Let's look at *ios/RCTVideo.h* (*https://github.com/react-native-community/react-native-video/blob/1.0.0/ios/RCTVideo.h*):

```
// RCTVideo.h
#import <React/RCTView.h>
#import <AVFoundation/AVFoundation.h>
#import "AVKit/AVKit.h"
#import "UIView+FindUIViewController.h"
#import "RCTVideoPlayerViewController.h"
#import "RCTVideoPlayerViewControllerDelegate.h"

@class RCTEventDispatcher;

@interface RCTVideo : UIView <RCTVideoPlayerViewControllerDelegate>
```

```
@property (nonatomic, copy) RCTBubblingEventBlock onVideoLoadStart;
// ...
// ...more properties omitted here...
// ...

- (instancetype)initWithEventDispatcher:
  (RCTEventDispatcher *)eventDispatcher NS_DESIGNATED_INITIALIZER;

- (AVPlayerViewController*)createPlayerViewController:
    (AVPlayer*)player withPlayerItem:(AVPlayerItem*)playerItem;

@end
```

This time, instead of subclassing NSObject, RCTVideo subclasses UIView. That makes sense because it's rendering a view component.

If we look at the implementation file, *RCTVideo.m* (*https://github.com/react-native-community/react-native-video/blob/1.0.0/ios/RCTVideo.m*), there's *a lot* going on. At the top are instance variables, keeping track of things like volume, playback rate, and the AVPlayer itself:

```
- (AVPlayerViewController*)
    createPlayerViewController: (AVPlayer*)player
    withPlayerItem:(AVPlayerItem*)playerItem
  {
    RCTVideoPlayerViewController* playerLayer =
      [[RCTVideoPlayerViewController alloc] init];
    playerLayer.showsPlaybackControls = NO;
    playerLayer.rctDelegate = self;
    playerLayer.view.frame = self.bounds;
    playerLayer.player = _player;
    playerLayer.view.frame = self.bounds;
    return playerLayer;
  }
```

There are also various methods for things like calculating the duration of the video, loading in the video and setting it as the source, and more. Feel free to step through these methods and figure out what role they play.

The other piece of the puzzle is the RCTVideoManager. To create a native UI component, as opposed to just a module, we also need a view manager. As the name implies, while the view actually handles rendering logic and similar tasks, the view manager deals with other stuff (event handling, property exports, etc.). At a minimum, the view manager class needs to:

- Subclass RCTViewManager
- Use the RCT_EXPORT_MODULE() macro
- Implement the -(UIView *)view method

The view method should return a UIView instance. In this case, we can see that it instantiates and returns an RCTVideo:

```
- (UIView *)view
{
  return [[RCTVideo alloc]
    initWithEventDispatcher:self.bridge.eventDispatcher];
}
```

The RCTVideoManager also exports a number of properties and constants:

```
#import "RCTVideoManager.h"
#import "RCTVideo.h"
#import <React/RCTBridge.h>
#import <AVFoundation/AVFoundation.h>

@implementation RCTVideoManager

RCT_EXPORT_MODULE();

@synthesize bridge = _bridge;

- (UIView *)view
{
  return [[RCTVideo alloc]
    initWithEventDispatcher:self.bridge.eventDispatcher];
}

- (dispatch_queue_t)methodQueue
{
    return dispatch_get_main_queue();
}

RCT_EXPORT_VIEW_PROPERTY(src, NSDictionary);
RCT_EXPORT_VIEW_PROPERTY(resizeMode, NSString);
RCT_EXPORT_VIEW_PROPERTY(repeat, BOOL);
RCT_EXPORT_VIEW_PROPERTY(paused, BOOL);
RCT_EXPORT_VIEW_PROPERTY(muted, BOOL);
RCT_EXPORT_VIEW_PROPERTY(controls, BOOL);
RCT_EXPORT_VIEW_PROPERTY(volume, float);
RCT_EXPORT_VIEW_PROPERTY(playInBackground, BOOL);
RCT_EXPORT_VIEW_PROPERTY(playWhenInactive, BOOL);
RCT_EXPORT_VIEW_PROPERTY(rate, float);
/* ... more RCT_EXPORT_VIEW_PROPERTY calls omitted here... */

- (NSDictionary *)constantsToExport
{
  return @{
    @"ScaleNone": AVLayerVideoGravityResizeAspect,
    @"ScaleToFill": AVLayerVideoGravityResize,
    @"ScaleAspectFit": AVLayerVideoGravityResizeAspect,
    @"ScaleAspectFill": AVLayerVideoGravityResizeAspectFill
  };
```

```
}

@end
```

Together, `RCTVideo` and `RCTVideoManager` comprise the `RCTVideo` native UI component, which we can use freely from within our application. As you can see, writing
native modules that make use of the iOS SDK is a nontrivial endeavor, though not an
insurmountable one. This is definitely one area where previous iOS development
experience will serve you well. A full explanation of iOS development is beyond the
scale of this book, but by looking at others' native modules—even if you don't have
much Objective-C experience—you should be able to start experimenting with your
own attempts at native module development.

Java Native Modules

Native modules for Android behave similarly to native modules for iOS. You can find
more information about Android native modules in the docs (*http://bit.ly/1kQ3STm*).

Just as with iOS, if you install a module for Android that includes native code, you'll
want to run `react-native link` after adding the module to your application's *pack-
age.json* file.

Writing a Java Native Module for Android

In order to better understand how Java native modules work, we'll write our own. Just
like with Objective-C, we'll start with a simpe "Hello, World" module.

We'll begin by making a directory for our `HelloWorld` package. It should be a sibling
to *MainActivity.java*. Android projects have a pretty deep nesting structure! Note that
the directory structure may vary between different versions of Android and React
Native. The key is that your new directory needs to be in the same directory as *Main-
Activity.java*.

```
mkdir android/app/src/main/java/com/depends/helloworld
```

Now we'll add a *HelloWorldModule.java* file to that directory, as shown in
Example 7-6.

Example 7-6. helloworld/HelloWorldModule.java

```
package com.depends.helloworld;

import android.util.Log;
import com.facebook.react.bridge.ReactContextBaseJavaModule;
import com.facebook.react.bridge.ReactApplicationContext;
import com.facebook.react.bridge.ReactMethod;
```

```
public class HelloWorldModule extends ReactContextBaseJavaModule {
  public HelloWorldModule(ReactApplicationContext reactContext) {
    super(reactContext);
  }

  @Override
  public String getName() {
    return "HelloWorld";
  }

  @ReactMethod
  public void greeting(String message) {
    Log.e("HelloWorldModule", "Saluton, " + message);
  }
}
```

There's quite a bit of boilerplate here. Let's take this piece by piece.

First, we begin with a `package` statement:

```
package com.depends.helloworld;
```

This is based on the file's location in the directory.

Next, we import several React Native–specific files, as well as *android.util.Log*. Any module you write should import the same React Native files.

Then we declare our `HelloWorldModule` class. It's public, meaning that external files can use it; and it extends the `ReactContextBaseJavaModule`, meaning that it inherits methods from `ReactContextBaseJavaModule`:

```
public class HelloWorldModule extends ReactContextBaseJavaModule { ... }
```

There are three methods implemented here: `HelloWorldModule`, `getName`, and `greeting`.

In Java, a method with the same name as the class is called the *constructor*. The `HelloWorldModule` method is thus a bit of boilerplate; we invoke the `ReactContextBaseJavaModule` constructor with a call to `super(reactContext)` and don't do anything else.

`getName` determines which name we'll use later on to access this module from our JavaScript code, so make sure it's correct! In this case, we name it "HelloWorld." Note that we add an `@Override` decorator here. You'll want to implement `getName` for any other modules you write.

Finally, `greeting` is our own method, which we want to be available in our JavaScript code. We add a `@ReactMethod` decorator so that React Native knows this method should be exposed. To log something when `greeting` is called, we call `Log.e` like so:

```
    Log.e("HelloWorldModule", "Hello, " + name);
```

The Log object in Android provides different levels of logging. The three most commonly used are INFO, WARN, and ERROR, and are invoked with Log.i, Log.w, and Log.e, respectively. Each of these methods takes in two parameters: the "tag" for your log, and the message. It's standard practice to use the class name for the tag. View the Android documentation (*http://bit.ly/1MxTUiq*) for more details.

We also need to create a package file to wrap this module (Example 7-7) so that we can include it in our build. It should also be a sibling to *HelloWorldModule.java*.

Example 7-7. helloworld/HelloWorldPackage.java

```java
package com.depends.helloworld;

import com.facebook.react.ReactPackage;
import com.facebook.react.bridge.JavaScriptModule;
import com.facebook.react.bridge.NativeModule;
import com.facebook.react.bridge.ReactApplicationContext;
import com.facebook.react.uimanager.ViewManager;

import java.util.ArrayList;
import java.util.Collections;
import java.util.List;

public class HelloWorldPackage implements ReactPackage {
  @Override
  public List<NativeModule>
    createNativeModules(ReactApplicationContext reactContext) {
    List<NativeModule> modules = new ArrayList<>();
    modules.add(new HelloWorldModule(reactContext));
    return modules;
  }

  @Override public List<ViewManager>
    createViewManagers(ReactApplicationContext reactContext) {
    return Collections.emptyList();
  }
}
```

This file is mostly boilerplate. We don't need to import HelloWorld because it's part of the same package (com.depends.helloworld) as this file. There are two methods that we need to implement: createNativeModules and createViewManagers. React Native uses these methods to determine what modules it should export.

Our native module doesn't deal with native views or UI elements so createViewManagers returns an empty list, whereas createNativeModules returns a list containing an instance of HelloWorld.

Finally, we need to add the package in *MainApplication.java*. Import the package file:

```
import com.depends.helloworld.HelloWorldPackage;
```

Then add `HelloWorldPackage` to `getPackages()`:

```
protected List<ReactPackage> getPackages() {
  return Arrays.<ReactPackage>asList(
      new MainReactPackage(),
      new ReactVideoPackage(),
      new HelloWorldPackage()
  );
}
```

Just like with Objective-C modules, our Java module will be available via the `React.NativeModules` object. We can now invoke our `greeting()` method from anywhere within our app, like so:

```
import { NativeModules } from "react-native";
NativeModules.HelloWorld.greeting("Bonnie");
```

Let's filter the logs and look for our message. Run the following from your project's root:

adb logcat

You will need to restart the application in order to see the log message output.

react-native run-android

Figure 7-6 shows the output you should see in your shell.

```
10-11 14:01:45.081  2335  2369 I HelloWorld: Hello, Bonnie
10-11 14:01:45.081  2335  2369 I HelloWorld: Hello, Bonnie
```

Figure 7-6. Output from logcat

Now that we've written our "Hello, World" example from Java, let's look at the implementation of `react-native-video` for Android.

Exploring react-native-video for Java

`react-native-video` for Android is basically a wrapper around the `MediaPlayer` API. It consists mainly of three files:

- *ReactVideoView.java*
- *ReactVideoPackage.java*
- *ReactVideoViewManager.java*

The *ReactVideoPackage.java* file, shown in Example 7-8, looks very similar to our *HelloWorldPackage.java* file.

Example 7-8. ReactVideoPackage.java

```java
package com.brentvatne.react;

import android.app.Activity;
import com.facebook.react.ReactPackage;
import com.facebook.react.bridge.JavaScriptModule;
import com.facebook.react.bridge.NativeModule;
import com.facebook.react.bridge.ReactApplicationContext;
import com.facebook.react.uimanager.ViewManager;

import java.util.Arrays;
import java.util.Collections;
import java.util.List;

public class ReactVideoPackage implements ReactPackage {

    @Override
    public List<NativeModule> createNativeModules(
      ReactApplicationContext reactContext) {
        return Collections.emptyList();
    }

    @Override
    public List<ViewManager> createViewManagers(
      ReactApplicationContext reactContext
    ) {
        return Arrays.<ViewManager>asList(
          new ReactVideoViewManager()
        );
    }
}
```

The main difference is that `ReactVideoPackage` returns `ReactVideoViewManager` from `createViewManagers`, while our `HelloWorldPackage` returned `HelloWorld` from `createNativeModules`. What's the difference?

For Android, any natively rendering views are created and controlled by a `ViewManager` (or, more specifically, a class that extends `ViewManager`). Because `React VideoView` is a UI component, we need to return a `ViewManager`. The React Native documentation on native Android UI components (*https://facebook.github.io/react-native/docs/native-components-android.html*) has some more information on the difference between exposing a native module (i.e., nonrendering Java code) and a UI component.

Let's look at *ReactVideoViewManager.java* next. It's a relatively long file; you can view the full source in the `react-native-linear-gradient` GitHub repo (*http://bit.ly/ RVVMFull*). Example 7-9 shows an abbreviated version.

Example 7-9. ReactVideoViewManager.java, abbreviated

```java
public class ReactVideoViewManager
  extends SimpleViewManager<ReactVideoView> {

    public static final String REACT_CLASS = "RCTVideo";

    public static final String PROP_VOLUME = "volume";
    public static final String PROP_SEEK = "seek";
    /** more props skipped here ... **/

    @Override
    public String getName() {
        return REACT_CLASS;
    }

    @Override
    protected ReactVideoView createViewInstance(
      ThemedReactContext themedReactContext
    ) {
        return new ReactVideoView(themedReactContext);
    }

    @Override
    public void onDropViewInstance(ReactVideoView view) {
        super.onDropViewInstance(view);
        view.cleanupMediaPlayerResources();
    }

    /** more methods skipped here ... **/

    @ReactProp(name = PROP_VOLUME, defaultFloat = 1.0f)
    public void setVolume(
      final ReactVideoView videoView,
      final float volume
    ) {
        videoView.setVolumeModifier(volume);
    }

    @ReactProp(name = PROP_SEEK)
    public void setSeek(
      final ReactVideoView videoView,
      final float seek
    ) {
        videoView.seekTo(Math.round(seek * 1000.0f));
    }
}
```

There are a few things we should pay attention to here.

The first is the implementation of getName. Note that, just as in our HelloWorld example, we need to implement getName in order to be able to refer to this component from our JavaScript code.

The next is the setVolume method and the use of the @ReactProp decorator. Here we declare that the <Video> component will take a prop named volume (as that's the value of PROP_VOLUME) and setVolume will be invoked when that prop changes. In setVolume, we check to see that the underlying view exists; if it does, we pass the colors along so that it can update. There are many methods in the implementation of ReactVideoViewManager that follow this pattern.

Finally, in createViewInstance, ReactVideoViewManager handles actually creating the view with the correct context.

In order to effectively write native Android components, you'll want an understanding of how Android handles views in general, but looking at other React Native components is a good place to start.

Cross-Platform Native Modules

Is it possible to write a cross-platform native module?

The answer is yes; you just have to implement your module separately for each platform, and provide a unified JavaScript interface. This can be a good way to handle platform-specific optimizations while still maximizing code reuse.

Creating a cross-platform native module doesn't require much extra configuration. Once you have implemented iOS and Android versions separately, just create a folder containing *index.ios.js* and *index.android.js* files. Each version should import the appropriate native module. Then you can import that folder, and React Native will pick up the platform-appropriate version.

React Native won't enforce a consistent API between the iOS and Android versions, so that responsibility falls on you. If you want the iOS and Android versions to have slightly different APIs, that's fine, too.

Summary

So, when is it appropriate to use native Objective-C or Java code? When is it a good idea to include third-party modules and libraries? In general, there are three main use cases for native modules: taking advantage of existing Objective-C or Java code; writing high-performance, multithreaded code for tasks such as graphics processing; and exposing APIs not yet included in React Native.

For any existing mobile projects built in Objective-C or Java, writing a native module can be a great way to reuse existing code in React Native applications. While hybrid applications are a bit beyond the scope of this book, they're definitely a feasible approach, and you can use native modules to share functionality between JavaScript, Objective-C, and Java.

Similarly, for use cases where performance is critical or for specialized tasks, it often makes sense to work in the native language of the platform you're developing for. In these cases, you can do the heavy lifting in Objective-C or Java and then pass the result back to your JavaScript application.

Finally, there will inevitably be platform APIs you'll want to use that aren't yet supported by React Native. In these cases, you have two options. One is to turn to the community and hope that someone else has already solved your problem. The other is to solve the issue yourself, and hopefully contribute your solution back to the community! Being able to write your own native modules means that you don't need to rely on React Native core in order to take advantage of your host platform.

Even if you've never developed for iOS or Android before, if you're planning on developing with React Native, it's a good idea to try to gain a reading knowledge of Objective-C and/or Java. If you hit a wall when working with React Native, being able to try to dig your way around it is a really invaluable asset. Don't be afraid to try!

The React Native community, as well as the broader JavaScript ecosystem, will be valuable resources as you develop your own React Native applications. Build on the work of others, and reach out if you need help.

Platform-Specific Code

In Chapter 7 we looked at how to write native modules with separate implementations in Java and Objective-C. This raises two questions: first, do all React Native components have implementations on both iOS and Android? Should they? How should you handle platform-specific implementations in your own code?

Not all components are available on all platforms, and not all interaction patterns are appropriate for all devices. That doesn't mean you can't use platform-specific code in your application, though! In this section, we'll cover platform-specific interface and implementations, as well as strategies for how to incorporate platform-specific components into your cross-platform applications.

 Writing cross-platform code in React Native is not an all-or-nothing endeavor: you can mix cross-platform and platform-specific code in your application, as we'll do in this section.

iOS- or Android-Only Components

Some components are available only on a specific platform. This includes things like `<TabBarIOS>` or `<ToolbarAndroid>`. They're usually platform-specific because they wrap some kind of underlying platform-specific API. For some components, having a platform-agnostic version doesn't make sense. For instance, the `<ToolbarAndroid>` component exposes an Android-specific API for a view type that doesn't exist on iOS anyway.

Platform-specific components are named with an appropriate suffix: either `IOS` or `Android`. If you try to include one on the wrong platform, your application will crash.

Components can also have platform-specific props. These are tagged in the documentation with a small badge indicating their usage. For instance, `<TextInput>` has some props that are platform-agnostic and others that are specific to iOS or Android (Figure 8-1).

ios **maxLength** number

Limits the maximum number of characters that can be entered. Use this instead of implementing the logic in JS to avoid flicker.

android **numberOfLines** number

Sets the number of lines for a TextInput. Use it with multiline set to true to be able to fill the lines.

Figure 8-1. <TextInput> has Android and iOS-specific props

Components with Platform-Specific Implementations

So, how do you handle platform-specific components or props in a cross-platform application? The good news is that you can still use these components. By including them inside another component with a platform-specific implementation, you'll be able to render the appropriate content for each platform your app is designed for.

 A platform-specific *component* works only on a specific platform. For example, `<ToolbarAndroid>` is Android-only. A component with platform-specific *implementation* might work on several platforms but may be implemented and behave differently.

A very common practice is to have a parent component that "wraps" platform-specific behavior and presents a unified API. For elements such as navigation UI, this makes a lot of sense; the interaction patterns vary greatly between iOS and Android.

In this section, we'll discuss how to implement platform-specific behavior in your components.

Using Platform-Specific File Extensions

Remember how React Native applications are initialized with both an *index.ios.js* and an *index.android.js* file? This naming convention can be used for any file to create a component that has different implementations on Android and iOS.

Example 8-1 demonstrates the Android implementation of a simple component that shows a pop-up message.

Example 8-1. Newsflash.android.js

```
import React from "react";
import { StyleSheet, Text, View, Alert } from "react-native";

export default class App extends React.Component {
  componentDidMount() {
    Alert.alert("Hey!", "You're on Android.");
  }

  render() {
    return (
      <View style={styles.container}>
        <Text>
          What? I didn't say anything.
        </Text>
      </View>
    );
  }
}

const styles = StyleSheet.create({
  container: {
    flex: 1,
    backgroundColor: "#fff",
    alignItems: "center",
    justifyContent: "center"
  }
});
```

And Example 8-2 shows the iOS version.

Example 8-2. Newsflash.ios.js

```
import React from "react";
import { StyleSheet, Text, View, Alert } from "react-native";

export default class App extends React.Component {
  componentDidMount() {
    Alert.alert("Hey!", "You're on iOS.");
  }

  render() {
    return (
      <View style={styles.container}>
        <Text>
          What? I didn't say anything.
        </Text>
      </View>
    );
  }
```

```
}

const styles = StyleSheet.create({
  container: {
    flex: 1,
    backgroundColor: "#fff",
    alignItems: "center",
    justifyContent: "center"
  }
});
```

Example 8-2 looks almost identical to Example 8-1, and it implements the same API. These files need to be located in the same directory.

To import this component, we use:

```
import Newsflash from "./Newsflash";
```

Note that we left off the file extension. The React Native packager will look for the appropriate file extension to match the platform. On iOS, it will load *Newsflash.ios.js* (see Figure 8-2). On Android, it will load *Newsflash.android.js*.

And, just like that, we have a cross-platform component that is compatible with both iOS and Android but that renders differently according to the platform.

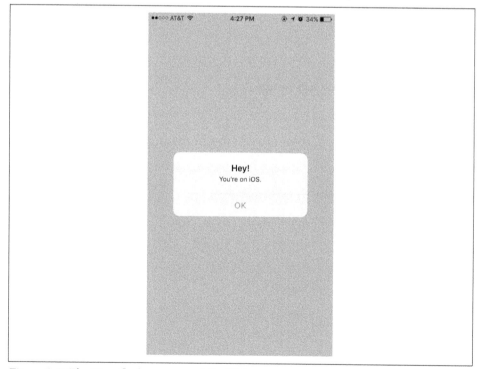

Figure 8-2. The Newsflash component for iOS

Using the Platform Module

There's a second option for writing platform-specific code: the Platform module. This API provides information about the operating system and OS version that your application is running on.

```
import { Platform } from "react-native";

console.log("What OS am I using?");
console.log(Platform.OS);

console.log("What version of the OS?");
console.log(Platform.Version); // e.g., 25 for Android Nougat
```

The Platform API can be useful when you want to adjust a few elements based on the platform but don't want to write fully separate component implementations. One common use case is for stylesheets, such as when you have different color schemes for different platforms.

```
import { Platform, StyleSheet } from "react-native";

const styles = StyleSheet.create({
  color: (Platform.OS === "ios") ? "#FF6666" : "#DD4444",
});
```

When to Use Platform-Specific Components

When is it appropriate to use a platform-specific component? In most cases, you'll want to do so when there's a platform-specific interaction pattern that you want your application to adhere to. If you want your application to feel truly "native," it's worth paying attention to platform-specific UI norms.

Apple and Google both provide human interface guidelines for their platforms which are worth consulting:

- iOS Human Interface Guidelines (*http://bit.ly/designing_for_ios*)
- Android Design Reference (*http://bit.ly/android_design_reference*)

By creating platform-specific versions of only certain components, you can strike a balance between code reuse and platform-based customization. In most cases, you should only need separate implementations of a handful of components in order to support both iOS and Android.

Debugging and Developer Tools

As you develop your own applications, chances are that something will go wrong along the way. When it's time to debug your applications, we happily have some React Native–specific tools that will make the job easier. There are also some nasty bugs that can crop up at the intersection of React Native and its host platform. In this chapter, we'll dig into the common pitfalls of React Native development and the tools you can use to tackle them. And because any discussion of debugging would be incomplete without reference to testing, we'll also cover the basics of getting automated testing set up for your React Native code.

JavaScript Debugging Practices, Translated

When working with React for the web, we have a number of common JavaScript-based tools and techniques to help us debug our applications. Most of these are also available for React Native, though occasionally with some minor adjustments. React Native gives us access to the console, debugger, and React developer tools that we're accustomed to using, so debugging JavaScript-based issues in React Native should feel familiar.

Activating the Developer Options

In order to avail yourself of these tools, you'll need to enable Chrome Developer Tools in the in-app developer menu (Figure 9-1). You can access this menu by shaking the device. In the iOS simulator, you can access the menu by pressing Command +D. In an Android emulator, you can press Command+M (if on Mac) or Control+M (if on Windows). From there, you can select Debug in Chrome to enable the Chrome Developer Tools.

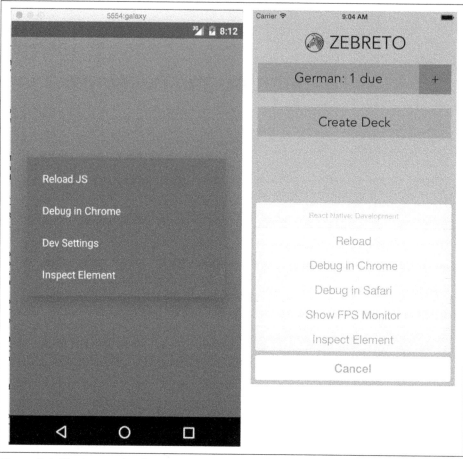

Figure 9-1. The in-app developer menu, as viewed from Android (left) and iOS (right)

Note that the developer menu is disabled in production builds.

If you're using an Expo app (i.e., one created with Create React Native App), the same shortcuts will open the Expo developer menu (see Figure 9-2).

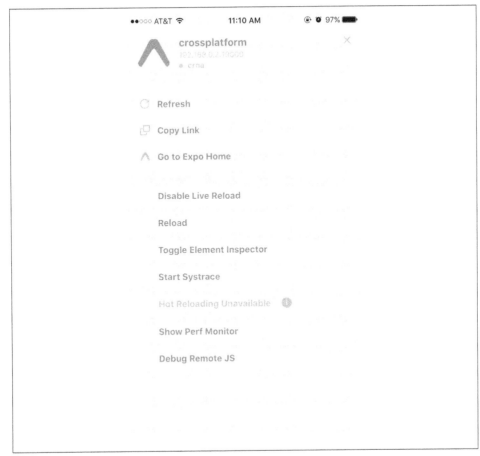

Figure 9-2. Expo developer menu

Debugging with console.log

One of the most basic, and common, forms of debugging is the "print it out and see what's happening" tactic. For many web-based developers, being able to add `console.log` to our code is an almost unconscious part of our workflow.

The JavaScript console works straight out of the box with React Native; you don't need to do any special configuration in order to use your `print` statements.

When using Xcode, you will see your console statements as output in the Xcode console (Figure 9-3). Note that you can expand how much room is allotted to the console by tweaking the visible Xcode panes.

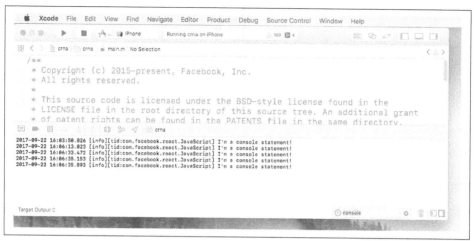

Figure 9-3. Console output as viewed in Xcode

Similarly, for Android, you can view the logs for your device by running `logcat` from your project's root (Figure 9-4 shows the output):

```
adb logcat
```

```
10-11 20:12:10.139  2070  2085 E Surface : getSlotFromBufferLocked: unknown buffer: 0xab751700
10-11 20:12:10.368  1282  1301 W AppOps  : Finishing op nesting under-run: uid 10058 pkg com.androiddepends code 24 time=0 duration=0 nesting=0
10-11 20:12:10.440  2070  2104 W ReactNativeJS: 'Warning: Native component for "RCTModalHostView" does not exist'
10-11 20:12:10.528  2070  2104 D ReactNativeJS: 'Running application "AndroidDepends" with appParams: {"initialProps":{},"rootTag":1}. __DEV__ === true, devel
opment-level warning are ON, performance optimizations are OFF'
10-11 20:12:10.529  1282  1293 W InputMethodManagerService: Window already focused, ignoring focus gain of: com.android.internal.view.IInputMethodClient$Stub$
Proxy@c707531 attribute=null, token = android.os.BinderProxy@e14a28e
10-11 20:12:10.542  2070  2104 D ReactNativeJS: 'CONSOLE.LOG IN LOGCAT'
```

Figure 9-4. Console output appears with the tag of "ReactNativeJS" in logcat

However, these views are rather cluttered, and also include logging related to platform-specific things. Console output is tagged with `ReactNativeJS`, so we can instead run:

```
adb logcat | grep ReactNativeJS
```

We can hop over into the browser-based developer tools for a more familiar—and cleaner—experience. Activate the developer menu and select Debug Remote JS, and then open the console in your web browser. As shown in Figure 9-5, you will be able to see the console output from the Chrome developer tools.

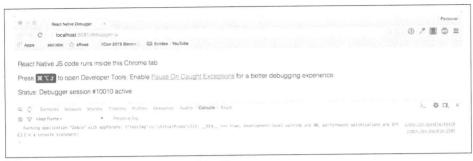

Figure 9-5. Console output as viewed in Chrome

Note that you need to open the console before you'll see things appear here.

How does this work? When you load your React Native application with remote Java-Script debugging enabled, the browser loads your React Native JavaScript code from the React Native packager using a standard `<script>` tag, so that you have full browser-based debugging control. The packager then uses WebSockets to communicate between the device and the browser.

We don't need to be too concerned with the specifics; we just need to know how to take advantage of these tools!

In addition to using `console.log`, you can also utilize `console.warn` or `con sole.error`. In developer builds, `console.warn` will display a yellow box at the bottom of your application, while messages from `console.error` will display a full-screen red message. These visual indicators will be disabled in production builds so you don't need to worry about them being displayed to end users.

Using the JavaScript Debugger

You can also use the JavaScript debugger just as you normally would for web-based React development. Open up the developer tools in Chrome and switch to the source tab, and then your breakpoints will be activated. You can see this in action in Figure 9-6.

Note that, similar to the JavaScript console, if you don't already have the developer tools pane open, the debugger may not be activated on your breakpoints. Likewise, if you don't have Debug Remote JS enabled, the debugger will not be activated.

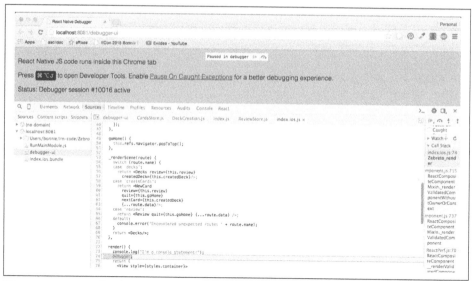

Figure 9-6. Using the debugger

When using the debugger, you have access to the usual view of your source code from within Chrome, and you can interact with the current JavaScript context via the in-browser console as well.

Working with the React Developer Tools

When you're developing with React for the web, the React developer tools are quite useful. They allow you to inspect the component hierarchy, examine the props and state of components, and modify the state from your browser. The React developer tools are available as a Chrome extension (*http://bit.ly/1O5DTlX*).

The React developer tools work with React Native as well. You'll need to install the standalone version to use them with React Native:

```
npm install -g react-devtools
```

Then launch the DevTools app, shown in Figure 9-7, by running:

```
react-devtools
```

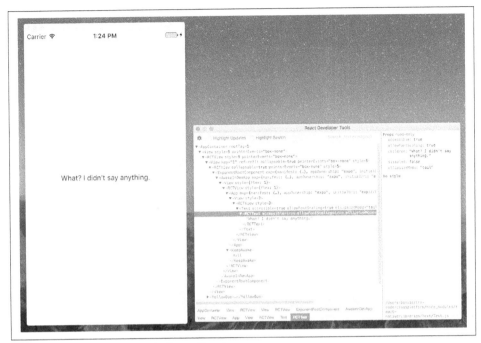

Figure 9-7. The React DevTools application

React Native Debugging Tools

In addition to the usual JavaScript-based web debugging tools, there are also some features specific to React Native that are relevant to debugging.

Using Inspect Element

While you can use the React developer tools via the browser, you may find that the "inspect element" functionality leaves something to be desired. However, there's also an in-app "inspect element" that you may find helpful. It has support for viewing things like style and gives you a quick way to dig through the component hierarchy. In Figure 9-8, you can see the result of inspecting a <Button> component.

Figure 9-8. Using Inspect Element will let you click on a component to view more information

This view also displays some basic performance metrics.

Interpreting the Red Screen of Death

One of the most common sights you'll see during application development is the Red Screen of Death. Alarming appearance aside, the Red Screen of Death is actually a boon: it takes errors and parses them into meaningful messages. So, learning to parse the information it displays is critical to an effective developer workflow.

For example, a syntax error might produce the output shown in Figure 9-9, indicating the file and line number where the error occurred.

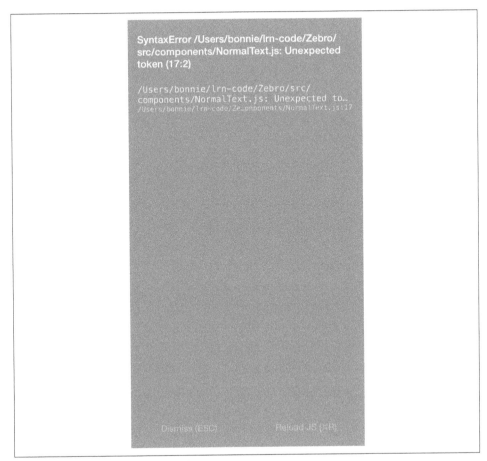

Figure 9-9. Red Screen of Death for a syntax error

Other common errors include attempting to use a variable without importing or defining it. For instance, a common issue is failing to explicitly import the <Text> component, like so:

```
import React, { Component } from "react";

export default class App extends Component {
  render() {
    return (
      <View>
        <Text>
          I haven't imported things properly!
        </Text>
      </View>
    );
  }
}
```

This results in the error message shown in Figure 9-10.

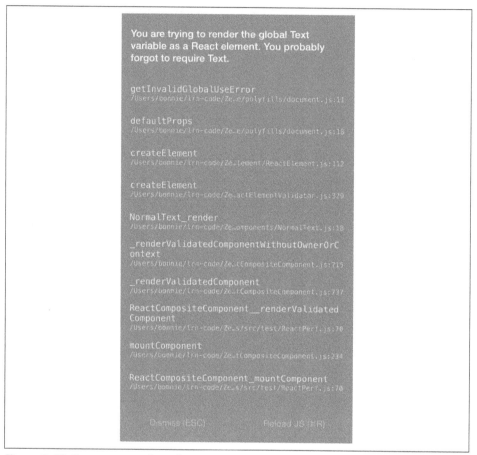

Figure 9-10. Error message from forgetting to import <Text>

Attempting to use an undeclared variable results in another error message (see Figure 9-11).

Figure 9-11. Error message from attempting to use an undeclared variable

Of particular use are the style-related error messages. For instance, if you pass in a bad value to a `StyleSheet.create` call, React Native will helpfully inform you which values would have been appropriate (see Figure 9-12).

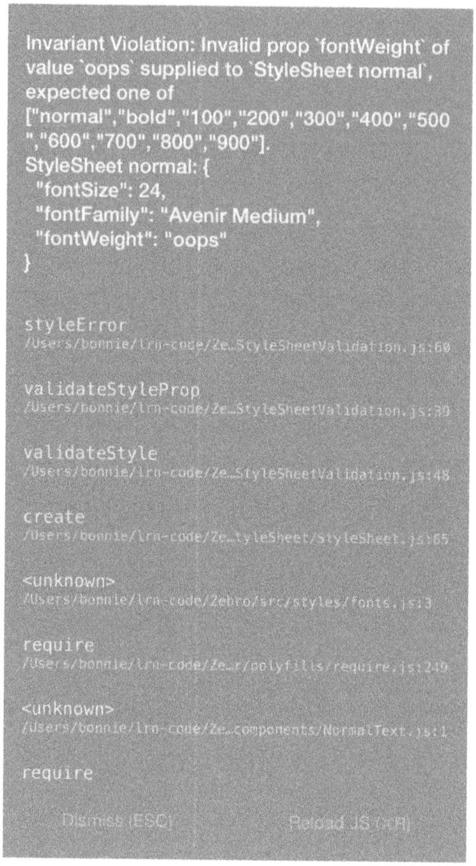

Figure 9-12. Error message from missetting a style property

While the Red Screen of Death may look alarming, it's really there to help you, and the error messages it presents are useful information. If for some reason you need to dismiss the screen, pressing the Escape key in the device simulator will take you back to your application.

Debugging Beyond JavaScript

As you write mobile applications with React Native, you will encounter errors not only in your React code but also in your application in general. If you are new to mobile development, these issues can be frustrating. Additionally, sometimes you'll see cryptic error messages and issues where your JavaScript codebase meets the host platform; the combination of host platform code and React Native can lead to confusing symptoms.

Learning to debug issues outside of pure JavaScript-based problems is critical to a productive development process with React Native. Happily, many of these issues are simpler than they might seem at first glance, and we have plenty of tools to help us along the way.

Common Development Environment Issues

Managing your developer environment for iOS, Android, and JavaScript can be a bit annoying, and it's not uncommon to encounter issues with any combination of the above.

If you encounter issues with the packager starting, or with building or running your application using `npm start` or `react-native run-android`, it's possible that you have a dependency problem.

If you're having dependency issues, one common solution is just to clean out your installed npm packages and reinstall them:

```
rm -rf node_modules
npm install
```

Common Xcode Problems

When you build your iOS application, if your application has any errors, they will appear in the Issues pane in Xcode (Figure 9-13). You can view them by selecting the warning icon.

Figure 9-13. Viewing the issues pane

Xcode will then point you to the relevant file and line number, and highlight the issue in the IDE. Figure 9-14 shows an example of a common error.

```
        // jsCodeLocation = [[NSBundle mainBundle] URLForResource:@"main" withExtension:@"jsbundle"];

  ⊘     RCTRootView *rootView = [[RCTRootView alloc] initWithBundleURL:jsCodeLocation
                                              moduleName:@"Zebro"    ⊘ No visible @interface for 'RCTRootView' declares the selector 'initWithBundleURL:moduleName:launchOptions:'
                                              launchOptions:launchOptions];
```

Figure 9-14. Interface error

This "No visible interface for RCTRootView" issue indicates that React Native's Objective-C classes are for some reason not visible to Xcode. In general, if you encounter "X is undefined" error messages in Xcode, where X is an RCT-prefixed class or otherwise part of React Native, it's a good idea to check on the packager and make sure that your JavaScript dependencies are in order:

1. Quit the packager.
2. Quit Xcode.
3. Run `npm install` from the project directory.
4. Reopen Xcode.

Another common problem deals with asset sizes (see Figure 9-15).

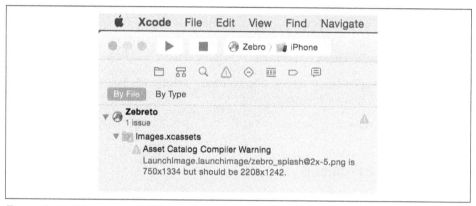

Figure 9-15. Warning regarding a missized image

Because assets should be sized appropriately for the device they're intended for (especially your application's icon), Xcode will throw a warning if you include an asset of an inappropriate size.

Deciphering Xcode's warnings may take some time at first, especially if you are unfamiliar with Objective-C. Some of the most confusing issues deal with the integration of React Native and your Xcode project, but doing a clean install of React Native usually clears up any problems.

Common Android Problems

When you run `react-native run-android`, some error messages may appear, preventing you from loading your application. The two most common issues are typically missing Android dependencies, or a failure to boot an Android Virtual Device (or plug in an eligible device via USB).

If you receive a warning about a missing package, run `android` and check to see if that package is listed as "installed." If not, install it. If it *is* installed but React Native can't find it, follow the steps just given to try to fix any issues with your development environment. You should also check to make sure that your ANDROID_HOME environment variable is properly set and points to your installation of the Android SDK. For example, on my system it looks like this:

```
$ echo $ANDROID_HOME
/usr/local/opt/android-sdk
```

If you receive a warning about no eligible device being available as a build target, check your device. Did you attempt to launch the emulator? If the emulator is still booting, the `react-native run-android` command will fail; give it a few seconds and try again. For a physical device, make sure that USB debugging is enabled.

You may also see issues after you create a signed version of your Android app:

```
$./gradlew installRelease
...
INSTALL_PARSE_FAILED_INCONSISTENT_CERTIFICATES:
New package has a different signature
```

You can solve this by uninstalling the old application from your device or emulator, and reattempting the installation. The error is caused by attempting to install an application with a different signing key—which happens after you generate your first signed APK.

The React Native Packager

Because React Native depends on the packager in order to rebuild your code, issues with the packager will manifest in problems fairly quickly.

The React Native packager will launch automatically when you run your project, either from Xcode or using `react-native run-android`. However, it will not quit automatically when you close your project. This means that if you switch projects, the packager will still be running—just from the wrong directory, so it will fail to compile your code. Always make sure that the packager is running from your project's root directory. You can launch it yourself with `npm start`.

If the React Native packager throws strange errors upon starting, chances are good that your development environment is in a bad state. Following the steps just described, make sure that your local installations of npm, Node, and react-native are all in a good state.

Issues Deploying to an iOS Device

When attempting to test your application on a real iOS device, you may encounter some peculiar issues.

If you are having trouble uploading to your iOS device, make sure that your device is selected correctly as the build target. Is your device of a supported type, based on your project settings? If your app explicitly disallows iPads, for instance, you won't be able to deploy to an iPad.

If you are using the React Native packager to rebuild your files as you make edits, you may see the screen shown in Figure 9-16.

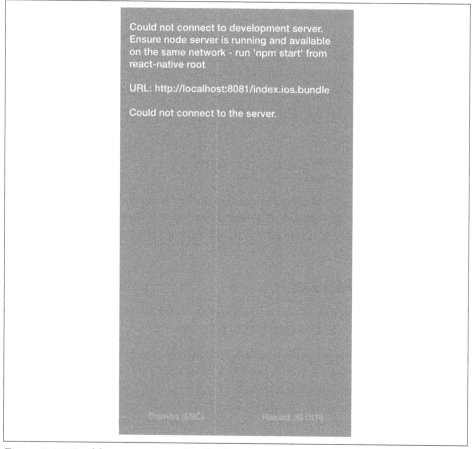

Could not connect to development server.
Ensure node server is running and available on the same network - run 'npm start' from react-native root

URL: http://localhost:8081/index.ios.bundle

Could not connect to the server.

Dismiss (ESC)   Reload JS (⌘R)

Figure 9-16. Could not connect to the development server

This indicates that your application has attempted to load its bundled JavaScript file from the React Native packager but is unable to do so. In this case, run through the following checks:

- Are your computer and iOS device on the same WiFi network?
- Is the React Native packager running from the project directory?

Simulator Behavior

You may also see strange behavior in the device simulator from time to time. If your application continues to crash repeatedly or it seems like changes to your code are not being reflected on the simulator, the easiest first step is to delete your application from the device.

Note that simply deleting your application may not have the desired effect; on many systems, your app may leave behind files that can cause side effects later on. As shown in Figure 9-17, the most straightforward way to start over with a clean slate on iOS is to reset the device simulator entirely, which removes *all* files and applications from the simulated device.

Figure 9-17. The Reset Content and Settings... option will delete everything from your device

Similarly, for Android emulators, you can delete the emulator and start over with a fresh device.

Testing Your Code

Debugging is all well and good, but you'll also want to prevent errors *before* they arise (and catch them when they inevitably do!). Automated tests and static type checking are useful tools that you'll probably want to make use of in your applications.

Testing JavaScript Code

Much of the React Native code you write may not even be aware that it's running in a mobile environment. For example, any business logic can probably be isolated from rendering logic. That means that you can test your JavaScript code using whatever tools you prefer for ordinary JavaScript development.

In this section, we're going to look specifically at type checking with Flow and unit testing with Jest.

Type Checking with Flow

Flow (*http://flowtype.org/*) is a JavaScript library for static type checking. It relies on type inference to detect type errors—even in unannotated code—and allows you to slowly add type annotations to existing projects. Type checking can help you detect possible issues early and helps you enforce sane APIs between various components and modules.

You can install Flow using npm:

```
$ npm install -g flow-bin
```

Running Flow is simple:

```
$ flow check
```

The default application comes with a *.flowconfig* file, which configures Flow's behavior. If you see many errors related to files in node_modules, you may need to add this line to your *.flowconfig* under [ignore]:

```
.*/node_modules/.*
```

You should then be able to run flow check without seeing any errors:

```
$ flow check
$ Found 0 errors.
```

Feel free to use Flow to assist you as you develop your React Native applications.

Unit Testing with Jest

React Native supports testing of React components using Jest. Jest is a unit testing framework built on top of Jasmine. It provides aggressive automocking of dependencies, and it meshes nicely with React's testing utilities.

To use Jest, you will first need to install it:

```
npm install jest-cli --save-dev
```

Because we only need Jest for development, not for our production build, we install it with the --save-dev flag.

Update your *package.json* file to include a test script:

```
{
  ...
  "scripts": {
    "test": "jest"
  }
```

```
        ...
    }
```

This will run jest when you type npm test.

Next, create the *tests/* directory. Jest will recursively search for files in a *tests/* directory, and run them:

```
mkdir __tests__
```

Now let's create a new file, *tests/dummy-test.js*, and write our first test:

```
'use strict';

describe('a silly test', function() {
  it('expects true to be true', function() {
    expect(true).toBe(true);
  });
});
```

Now if you run **npm test**, you should see that the test has passed.

Of course, there is much more to testing than this trivial example. If you want to read more about Jest, I recommend starting with the documentation (*https://face book.github.io/jest/*).

Snapshot Testing with Jest

Snapshot tests are excellent for ensuring that your UI does not change unexpectedly. This makes them a good fit for React components. Plus, snapshot tests are easy to write and require minimal configuration.

Snapshot testing for React Native requires the react-test-renderer package.

```
npm install --save react-test-renderer
```

Example 9-1 demonstrates a simple Jest test.

Example 9-1. Styles/tests/FlexDemo-test.js

```
import React from "react";
import FlexDemo from "../FlexDemo";

import renderer from "react-test-renderer";

test("renders correctly", () => {
  const tree = renderer.create(<FlexDemo />).toJSON();

  expect(tree).toMatchSnapshot();
});
```

As you can see, very little code is needed to add a snapshot test.

You'll also need to update your *package.json* file to add Jest as a dependency, with the `react-native` testing preset.

```
"dependencies": {
  ...
  "jest": "*"
  ...
},
"jest": {
  "preset": "react-native"
}
```

The first time you run `npm test`, a "snapshot" will be generated.

```
$ npm test
 PASS  __tests__/FlexDemo-test.js
  ✓ renders correctly (1216ms)

Snapshot Summary
 › 1 snapshot written in 1 test suite.
```

The snapshot file will look something like Example 9-2.

Example 9-2. The initial snapshot file

```
// Jest Snapshot v1, https://goo.gl/fbAQLP

exports[`renders correctly 1`] = `
<View
  style={
    Object {
      "alignItems": "flex-end",
      "backgroundColor": "#F5FCFF",
      "borderColor": "#0099AA",
      "borderWidth": 5,
      "flex": 1,
      "flexDirection": "row",
      "marginTop": 30,
    }
  }
>
  <Text
    accessible={true}
    allowFontScaling={true}
    ellipsizeMode="tail"
    style={
      Object {
        "borderColor": "#AA0099",
        "borderWidth": 2,
        "flex": 1,
```

```
        "fontSize": 24,
        "textAlign": "center",
      }
    }
  >
    Child One
</Text>
<Text
  accessible={true}
  allowFontScaling={true}
  ellipsizeMode="tail"
  style={
    Object {
      "borderColor": "#AA0099",
      "borderWidth": 2,
      "flex": 1,
      "fontSize": 24,
      "textAlign": "center",
    }
  }
>
    Child Two
</Text>
<Text
  accessible={true}
  allowFontScaling={true}
  ellipsizeMode="tail"
  style={
    Object {
      "borderColor": "#AA0099",
      "borderWidth": 2,
      "flex": 1,
      "fontSize": 24,
      "textAlign": "center",
    }
  }
  >
    Child Three
  </Text>
</View>
`;
```

Don't edit these files manually. Instead, when you update your application, run `npm test` again. If a component renders differently from the snapshot, Jest will fail and show you a diff between the expected and received version of the component:

```
$ npm test
 FAIL  __tests__/FlexDemo-test.js
  ● renders correctly

    expect(value).toMatchSnapshot()
```

```
Received value does not match stored snapshot 1.

- Snapshot
+ Received

@@ -41,22 +41,6 @@
        }
      }
    >
      Child Two
    </Text>
-   <Text
-     accessible={true}
-     allowFontScaling={true}
-     ellipsizeMode="tail"
-     style={
-       Object {
-         "borderColor": "#AA0099",
-         "borderWidth": 2,
-         "flex": 1,
-         "fontSize": 24,
-         "textAlign": "center",
-       }
-     }
-   >
-     Child Three
-   </Text>
  </View>

      at Object.<anonymous> (__tests__/FlexDemo-test.js:11:14)

  ✕ renders correctly (66ms)

Snapshot Summary
 › 1 snapshot test failed in 1 test suite.
```

When inspecting the diff, you can then decide whether or not the changes were in error or if you want to update your snapshot to reflect the changes. Snapshot files should be checked into source control.

When You're Stuck

If you end up with a particularly nasty problem that you can't solve on your own, you can try consulting the community. There are plenty of places to go to ask for advice:

- The #reactnative IRC chat (*irc.lc/freenode/reactnative*)
- The React discussion forum (*https://discuss.reactjs.org/*)
- StackOverflow (*http://stackoverflow.com/questions/tagged/react-native*)

If you suspect your issue may be a bug in React Native itself, check the existing list of issues on GitHub (*https://github.com/facebook/react-native/issues*). When you report issues, it's useful to create a small proof-of-concept application demonstrating the problem.

Summary

In general, debugging with React Native should feel quite similar to debugging your React code on the web. Most of the tools you are already familiar with are available here, too, which makes the transition to React Native much easier. That being said, React Native applications bring their own variety of complexity, and sometimes that complexity can manifest in frustrating bugs. Knowing how to debug your applications and becoming familiar with the error messages produced by your environment will go a long way in helping you to cultivate a productive workflow.

Navigation and Structure in Larger Applications

Now that we've covered many of the pieces you need to build your own React Native applications, let's put everything together. Up until now, we've mostly dealt with small examples. In this chapter, we'll look at the structure of a larger application. We'll cover how to use the `<StackNavigation>` component from `react-navigation` to handle transitions between different screens in an application.

The example application from this chapter will also be used in Chapter 11, where we'll look at how to integrate the state management library Redux into our application.

The Flashcard Application

In this chapter, we're going to be building a flashcard application that allows users to create decks of cards and then review them. The flashcard application is more complex than the sample applications we've been building so far. It's meant to model what a more fleshed-out application might look like. All the code is available on GitHub (*http://bit.ly/flashcardslrn*). This application is entirely JavaScript-based and cross-platform: it will work on iOS or Android, and is compatible with Expo (meaning you can use the Create React Native App).

As illustrated in Figure 10-1, the Flashcard app has three main views:

- The home page, which lists available decks and allows you to create new decks
- The card creation screen
- The review screen

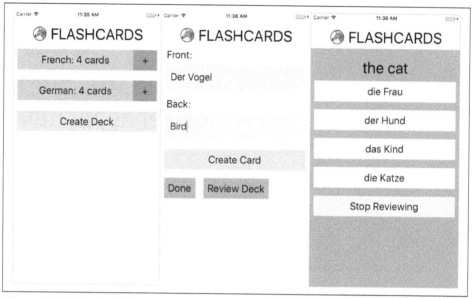

Figure 10-1. Viewing decks, card creation, and card review

Users of the app go through two main interaction flows. The first deals with content creation (i.e., the creation of decks as well as cards). The content creation process works as follows (illustrated in Figure 10-2):

1. The user taps Create Deck.

2. The user enters a deck name, then either taps the Return button or Create Deck again.

3. The user enters values for Front and Back, and then taps Create Card.

4. After entering zero or more cards, the user may tap Done, bringing him or her back to the original screen. Alternatively, the user may tap Review Deck and begin reviewing.

The user may also initiate card creation at a later date by tapping the + buttons on the home screen.

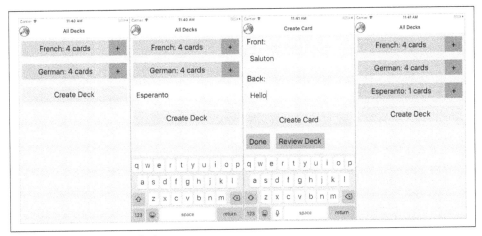

Figure 10-2. Creating a deck

The second main interaction flow deals with card review (illustrated in Figure 10-3):

1. The user taps the deck's name that he/she wishes to review.

2. The user is presented with the question screen.

3. The user taps one of the provided options.

4. The user receives feedback based on whether the guess was correct.

5. To view the next review, the user taps Continue.

6. Once all reviews are completed, the user reaches the "Reviews cleared!" screen.

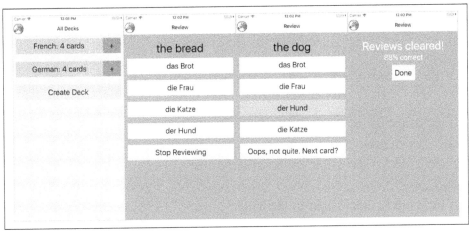

Figure 10-3. Reviewing cards

We'll be using the flashcard app, and in particular the features just described, to talk through some of the patterns and problems that emerge when building a more complete application.

Project Structure

Here's the structure of the flashcard application:

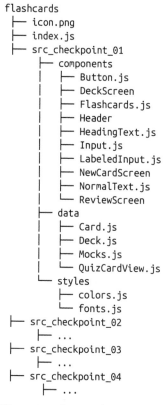

```
flashcards
├── icon.png
├── index.js
├── src_checkpoint_01
│   ├── components
│   │   ├── Button.js
│   │   ├── DeckScreen
│   │   ├── Flashcards.js
│   │   ├── Header
│   │   ├── HeadingText.js
│   │   ├── Input.js
│   │   ├── LabeledInput.js
│   │   ├── NewCardScreen
│   │   ├── NormalText.js
│   │   └── ReviewScreen
│   ├── data
│   │   ├── Card.js
│   │   ├── Deck.js
│   │   ├── Mocks.js
│   │   └── QuizCardView.js
│   └── styles
│       ├── colors.js
│       └── fonts.js
├── src_checkpoint_02
│   ├── ...
├── src_checkpoint_03
│   ├── ...
├── src_checkpoint_04
│   ├── ...
```

You'll notice that within the *flashcards* directory, there are actually four folders: *src_checkpoint_01*, *src_checkpoint_02*, *src_checkpoint_03*, and *src_checkpoint_04*. These each represent the state of the application as we work through the development process. We're going to begin with *src_checkpoint_01*.

components/
    All of our React components live here.

data/
    This is where you'll find our data models, representing cards, decks, and reviews.

---

styles/
Here you'll find stylesheet objects, which are reused elsewhere.

Application Screens

There are three main scenes that may be displayed at any given time.

First, we have deck creation, from the main deck screen. This screen will display as many decks as currently exist in the app, as shown in Figure 10-4.

Figure 10-4. Creating a deck from the main deck screen

In the code we're starting with, each of these screens is implemented as a component, but they aren't connected yet. If you try to interact with the application, it shows a "Not implemented" warning (see Figure 10-5).

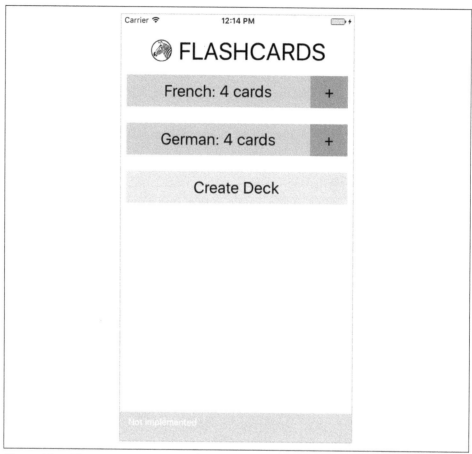

Figure 10-5. If you try to interact with the application, you get a warning

The root component for the application is located in *components/Flashcards.js* (see Example 10-1).

Example 10-1. src_checkpoint_01/components/Flashcards.js

```
import React, { Component } from "react";
import { StyleSheet, View } from "react-native";

import Heading from "./Header";
import DeckScreen from "./DeckScreen";
import NewCardScreen from "./NewCardScreen";
import ReviewScreen from "./ReviewScreen";

class Flashcards extends Component {
  _renderScene() {
    // return <ReviewScreen />;
```

```
    // return <NewCardScreen />;
    return <DeckScreen />;
  }
  render() {
    return (
      <View style={styles.container}>
        <Heading />
        {this._renderScene()}
      </View>
    );
  }
}
```

```
const styles = StyleSheet.create({ container: { flex: 1, marginTop: 30 } });
```

```
export default Flashcards;
```

The deck screen, card creation screen, and review screen are implemented as the <DeckScreen>, <NewCardScreen>, and <ReviewScreen> components, respectively.

<DeckScreen>, shown in Example 10-2, renders existing decks and a button for creating new decks.

Example 10-2. src_checkpoint_01/components/DeckScreen/index.js

```
import React, { Component } from "react";
import { View } from "react-native";

import { MockDecks } from "./../../../data/Mocks";
import Deck from "./Deck";
import DeckCreation from "./DeckCreation";

class DecksScreen extends Component {
  static displayName = "DecksScreen";

  constructor(props) {
    super(props);
    this.state = { decks: MockDecks };
  }

  _mkDeckViews() {
    if (!this.state.decks) {
      return null;
    }

    return this.state.decks.map(deck => {
      return <Deck deck={deck} count={deck.cards.length} key={deck.id} />;
    });
  }

  render() {
```

```
    return (
      <View>
        {this._mkDeckViews()}
        <DeckCreation />
      </View>
    );
  }
}

export default DecksScreen;
```

<NewCard>, shown in Example 10-3, has input fields for creating new cards. The call-
backs for handling actual card creation are not yet implemented.

Example 10-3. src_checkpoint_01/components/NewCardScreen/index.js

```
import React, { Component } from "react";
import { StyleSheet, View } from "react-native";

import DeckModel from "./../../data/Deck";

import Button from "../Button";
import LabeledInput from "../LabeledInput";
import NormalText from "../NormalText";
import colors from "./../../styles/colors";

class NewCard extends Component {
  constructor(props) {
    super(props);
    this.state = { font: "", back: "" };
  }

  _handleFront = text => {
    this.setState({ front: text });
  };

  _handleBack = text => {
    this.setState({ back: text });
  };

  _createCard = () => {
    console.warn("Not implemented");
  };

  _reviewDeck = () => {
    console.warn("Not implemented");
  };

  _doneCreating = () => {
    console.warn("Not implemented");
  };
```

```
  render() {
    return (
      <View>
        <LabeledInput
          label="Front"
          clearOnSubmit={false}
          onEntry={this._handleFront}
          onChange={this._handleFront}
        />
        <LabeledInput
          label="Back"
          clearOnSubmit={false}
          onEntry={this._handleBack}
          onChange={this._handleBack}
        />

        <Button style={styles.createButton} onPress={this._createCard}>
          <NormalText>Create Card</NormalText>
        </Button>

        <View style={styles.buttonRow}>
          <Button style={styles.secondaryButton} onPress={this._doneCreating}>
            <NormalText>Done</NormalText>
          </Button>

          <Button style={styles.secondaryButton} onPress={this._reviewDeck}>
            <NormalText>Review Deck</NormalText>
          </Button>
        </View>
      </View>
    );
  }
}

const styles = StyleSheet.create({
  createButton: { backgroundColor: colors.green },
  secondaryButton: { backgroundColor: colors.blue },
  buttonRow: { flexDirection: "row" }
});

export default NewCard;
```

<ReviewScreen>, shown in Example 10-4, displays a series of reviews in a multiple-choice style format. Once the user selects an answer, it renders the next review.

Example 10-4. src_checkpoint_01/components/ReviewScreen/index.js

```
import React, { Component } from "react";
import { StyleSheet, View } from "react-native";
```

```
import ViewCard from "./ViewCard";
import { MockReviews } from "./../../data/Mocks";
import { mkReviewSummary } from "./ReviewSummary";
import colors from "./../../styles/colors";

class ReviewScreen extends Component {
  static displayName = "ReviewScreen";

  constructor(props) {
    super(props);
    this.state = {
      numReviewed: 0,
      numCorrect: 0,
      currentReview: 0,
      reviews: MockReviews
    };
  }

  onReview = correct => {
    if (correct) {
      this.setState({ numCorrect: this.state.numCorrect + 1 });
    }
    this.setState({ numReviewed: this.state.numReviewed + 1 });
  };

  _nextReview = () => {
    this.setState({ currentReview: this.state.currentReview + 1 });
  };

  _quitReviewing = () => {
    console.warn("Not implemented");
  };

  _contents() {
    if (!this.state.reviews || this.state.reviews.length === 0) {
      return null;
    }

    if (this.state.currentReview < this.state.reviews.length) {
      return (
        <ViewCard
          onReview={this.onReview}
          continue={this._nextReview}
          quit={this._quitReviewing}
          {...this.state.reviews[this.state.currentReview]}
        />
      );
    } else {
      let percent = this.state.numCorrect / this.state.numReviewed;
      return mkReviewSummary(percent, this._quitReviewing);
    }
  }
}
```

```
  render() {
    return (
      <View style={styles.container}>
        {this._contents()}
      </View>
    );
  }
}

const styles = StyleSheet.create({
  container: { backgroundColor: colors.blue, flex: 1, paddingTop: 24 }
});

export default ReviewScreen;
```

You'll notice that many of the components used by these screens are not built-in React Native components, but rather reusable components provided for the purposes of building out the flashcard app. Let's take a look at them now.

Reusable Components

As mentioned earlier, when you're building larger applications it's useful to have some styled components that you can reuse over and over again. You may have noticed that the preceding components do not use <Text> in order to render text: instead, they use <HeadingText> and <NormalText>. Similarly, the <Button> component is reused frequently, as are the <Input> and <LabeledInput> components. This helps with code readability, makes creating new components easier, and makes it easy to restyle the application.

The following components are reusable components. We'll use them throughout the flashcard application as we flesh out the starter code and turn it into a working application.

The first of these components is a simple <Button>, shown in Example 10-5. It wraps an arbitrary component (i.e., this.props.children) in a <TouchableOpacity> component. It takes an onPress callback and also allows you to override the style via props.

Example 10-5. src_checkpoint_01/components/Button.js

```
import React, { Component } from "react";
import { StyleSheet, View, TouchableOpacity } from "react-native";

import colors from "./../styles/colors";

class Button extends Component {
  static displayName = "Button";
```

```
  render() {
    let opacity = this.props.disabled ? 1 : 0.5;
    return (
      <TouchableOpacity
        activeOpacity={opacity}
        onPress={this.props.onPress}
        style={[styles.wideButton, this.props.style]}
      >
        {this.props.children}
      </TouchableOpacity>
    );
  }
}

Button.defaultProps = { disabled: false };

export default Button;

const styles = StyleSheet.create({
  wideButton: {
    justifyContent: "center",
    alignItems: "center",
    padding: 10,
    margin: 10,
    backgroundColor: colors.pink
  }
});
```

Next up is the <NormalText> component, shown in Example 10-6. It's mostly an ordinary <Text> component with some styles applied to scale the font size based on the
window dimensions.

Example 10-6. src_checkpoint_01/components/NormalText.js

```
import React, { Component } from "react";
import { StyleSheet, Text, View } from "react-native";

import { fonts, scalingFactors } from "./../styles/fonts";
import Dimensions from "Dimensions";
let { width } = Dimensions.get("window");

class NormalText extends Component {
  static displayName = "NormalText";

  render() {
    return (
      <Text style={[this.props.style, fonts.normal, scaled.normal]}>
        {this.props.children}
      </Text>
    );
```

```
  }
}

const scaled = StyleSheet.create({
  normal: { fontSize: width * 1.0 / scalingFactors.normal }
});

export default NormalText;
```

<HeadingText>, shown in Example 10-7, is much the same as <NormalText>, but with a larger font size.

Example 10-7. src_checkpoint_01/components/HeadingText.js

```
import React, { Component } from "react";
import { StyleSheet, Text, View } from "react-native";

import { fonts, scalingFactors } from "./../styles/fonts";
import Dimensions from "Dimensions";
let { width } = Dimensions.get("window");

class HeadingText extends Component {
  static displayName = "HeadingText";

  render() {
    return (
      <Text style={[this.props.style, fonts.big, scaled.big]}>
        {this.props.children}
      </Text>
    );
  }
}

const scaled = StyleSheet.create({
  big: { fontSize: width / scalingFactors.big }
});

export default HeadingText;
```

<Input>, shown in Example 10-8, provides some sensible default props around the built-in <TextInput> component and handles updating state as well as triggering callbacks.

Example 10-8. src_checkpoint_01/components/Input.js

```
import React, { Component } from "react";
import { StyleSheet, TextInput, View } from "react-native";

import colors from "./../styles/colors";
import { fonts } from "./../styles/fonts";
```

```
class Input extends Component {
  constructor(props) {
    super(props);
    this.state = { text: "" };
  }

  _create = () => {
    this.props.onEntry(this.state.text);
    this.setState({ text: "" });
  };

  _onSubmit = ev => {
    this.props.onEntry(ev.nativeEvent.text);
    if (this.props.clearOnSubmit) {
      this.setState({ text: "" });
    }
  };

  _onChange = text => {
    this.setState({ text: text });
    if (this.props.onChange) {
      this.props.onChange(text);
    }
  };

  render() {
    return (
      <TextInput
        style={[
          styles.nameField,
          styles.wideButton,
          fonts.normal,
          this.props.style
        ]}
        ref="newDeckInput"
        multiline={false}
        autoCorrect={false}
        onChangeText={this._onChange}
        onSubmitEditing={this._onSubmit}
      />
    );
  }
}

// Default props are used if not otherwise specified
Input.defaultProps = { clearOnSubmit: true };

export default Input;

const styles = StyleSheet.create({
  nameField: { backgroundColor: colors.tan, height: 60 },
```

```
    wideButton: { justifyContent: "center", padding: 10, margin: 10 }
});
```

`<LabledInput>`, shown in Example 10-9, combines an `<Input>` with a `<NormalText>` component.

Example 10-9. src_checkpoint_01/components/LabeledInput.js

```
import React, { Component } from "react";

import { StyleSheet, View } from "react-native";

import Input from "./Input";
import NormalText from "./NormalText";

class LabeledInput extends Component {
  render() {
    return (
      <View style={styles.wrapper}>
        <NormalText style={styles.label}>
          {this.props.label}:
        </NormalText>
        <Input
          onEntry={this.props.onEntry}
          onChange={this.props.onChange}
          clearOnSubmit={this.props.clearOnSubmit}
          style={this.props.inputStyle}
        />
      </View>
    );
  }
}

const styles = StyleSheet.create({
  label: { paddingLeft: 10 },
  wrapper: { padding: 5 }
});

export default LabeledInput;
```

Styles

In addition to the reusable components, there are a couple of stylesheets located in the *styles* directory that are reused throughout the flashcard application. These files won't be modified as we develop the flashcard application.

The first, *fonts.js*, sets some default font sizes and colors (see Example 10-10).

Example 10-10. src_checkpoint_01/styles/fonts.js

```
import { StyleSheet } from "react-native";

export const fonts = StyleSheet.create({
  normal: { fontSize: 24 },
  alternate: { fontSize: 50, color: "#FFFFFF" },
  big: { fontSize: 32, alignSelf: "center" }
});

export const scalingFactors = { normal: 15, big: 10 };
```

The second, *colors.js*, defines some of the color values used in the application (see Example 10-11).

Example 10-11. src_checkpoint_01/styles/colors.js

```
export default (palette = {
  pink: "#FDA6CD",
  pink2: "#d35d90",
  green: "#65ed99",
  tan: "#FFEFE8",
  blue: "#5DA9E9",
  gray1: "#888888"
});
```

Data Models

Now that we've seen a bit about how our flashcard application handles rendering, how does it handle data? What data do we need to keep track of, and how do we do so?

We are concerned with two basic models: cards and decks. Reviews are constructed on the basis of cards and decks, but we won't need to store them. The following classes provide some convenient methods for working with decks and cards so that we don't need to deal with plain JavaScript objects.

The Deck class, shown in Example 10-12, lets you construct a deck based on a name. Each Deck contains an array of Cards. It also provides a convenience method for adding a card to a deck.

In Example 10-12, we're using the md5 module to generate simple IDs for cards and decks, based on their data.

Example 10-12. src_checkpoint_01/data/Deck.js

```
import md5 from "md5";
```

```javascript
class Deck {
  constructor(name) {
    this.name = name;
    this.id = md5("deck:" + name);
    this.cards = [];
  }

  setFromObject(ob) {
    this.name = ob.name;
    this.cards = ob.cards;
    this.id = ob.id;
  }

  static fromObject(ob) {
    let d = new Deck(ob.name);
    d.setFromObject(ob);
    return d;
  }

  addCard(card) {
    this.cards = this.cards.concat(card);
  }
}

export default Deck;
```

A card has two sides and belongs to a deck. The Card class is shown in Example 10-13.

Example 10-13. src_checkpoint_01/data/Card.js

```javascript
import md5 from "md5";

class Card {
  constructor(front, back, deckID) {
    this.front = front;
    this.back = back;
    this.deckID = deckID;
    this.id = md5(front + back + deckID);
  }

  setFromObject(ob) {
    this.front = ob.front;
    this.back = ob.back;
    this.deckID = ob.deckID;
    this.id = ob.id;
  }

  static fromObject(ob) {
    let c = new Card(ob.front, ob.back, ob.deckID);
    c.setFromObject(ob);
```

```
      return c;
  }
}

export default Card;
```

A `QuizCardView`, shown in Example 10-14, is really a partial review, comprising a question, several possible answers, and a correct answer, as well as the card's orientation (whether it's from English to Spanish or Spanish to English, for example). This class also includes a method for generating reviews from a set of cards.

Example 10-14. src_checkpoint_01/data/QuizCardView.js

```
import _ from "lodash";

class QuizCardView {
  constructor(orientation, cardID, prompt, correctAnswer, answers) {
    this.orientation = orientation;
    this.cardID = cardID;
    this.prompt = prompt;
    this.correctAnswer = correctAnswer;
    this.answers = answers;
  }
}

function mkReviews(cards) {
  let makeReviews = function(sideOne, sideTwo) {
    return cards.map(card => {
      let others = cards.filter(other => {
        return other.id !== card.id;
      });

      let answers = _.shuffle(
        [card[sideTwo]].concat(_.sampleSize(_.map(others, sideTwo), 3))
      );

      return new QuizCardView(
        sideOne,
        card.id,
        card[sideOne],
        card[sideTwo],
        answers
      );
    });
  };

  let reviews = makeReviews("front", "back").concat(
    makeReviews("back", "front")
  );
  return _.shuffle(reviews);
}
```

```
export { mkReviews, QuizCardView };
```

Finally, the Mocks class provides some mock data, which is useful for testing and developing our application (see Example 10-15).

Example 10-15. src_checkpoint_01/data/Mocks.js

```
import CardModel from "./Card";
import DeckModel from "./Deck";
import { mkReviews } from "./QuizCardView";

let MockCards = [
  new CardModel("der Hund", "the dog", "fakeDeckID"),
  new CardModel("das Kind", "the child", "fakeDeckID"),
  new CardModel("die Frau", "the woman", "fakeDeckID"),
  new CardModel("die Katze", "the cat", "fakeDeckID")
];

let MockCard = MockCards[0];
let MockReviews = mkReviews(MockCards);
let MockDecks = [new DeckModel("French"), new DeckModel("German")];

MockDecks.map(deck => {
  deck.addCard(new CardModel("der Hund", "the dog", deck.id));
  deck.addCard(new CardModel("die Katze", "the cat", deck.id));
  deck.addCard(new CardModel("das Brot", "the bread", deck.id));
  deck.addCard(new CardModel("die Frau", "the woman", deck.id));
  return deck;
});

let MockDeck = MockDecks[0];

export { MockReviews, MockCards, MockCard, MockDecks, MockDeck };
```

The files in the *data* directory won't change as we develop our flashcard application.

Using React-Navigation

Right now we have a skeletal application with much of the rendering taken care of, but it's not functional. Let's make it so that we can navigate through the app.

Mobile applications usually involve several screens and provide ways to transition between them. Navigation libraries handle those transitions and give developers a way to express the relationships between screens. There are several libraries available for use with React Native. We're going to use React Navigation, which is a library provided by the react-community GitHub project (*https://github.com/react-community*).

Creating a StackNavigator

Let's start by adding `react-navigation` to our project.

```
npm install --save react-navigation
```

React Navigation actually provides several *navigators*. Navigators render common, configurable UI elements, such as headers. They also determine your application's navigation structure. We're going to use the `StackNavigator`, which renders a single screen at a time and provides transitions between a "stack" of screens. This is probably the most common UI pattern for mobile applications.

Other navigators provided by React Navigation, such as the `TabNavigator` and the `DrawerNavigator`, provide slightly different perspectives on application structure. You can also combine several navigators within a single application.

For now, let's import the `StackNavigator` in *components/Flashcards.js*.

```
import { StackNavigator } from "react-navigation"
```

In order to use the `StackNavigator`, we need to create it with information about the available screens.

```
let navigator = StackNavigator({
  Home: { screen: DeckScreen },
  Review: { screen: ReviewScreen },
  CardCreation: { screen: NewCardScreen }
});
```

Then, instead of exporting the `<Flashcards>` component from *Flashcards.js*, we can export the navigator.

```
export default navigator;
```

Using navigation.navigate to Transition Between Screens

What does creating a `StackNavigator` get us? Well, now each screen included in the `StackNavigator` will be rendered with a special `navigation` prop. If we call:

```
this.props.navigation.navigate("SomeRoute");
```

The navigator will attempt to find the appropriately named screen to render.

Additionally, we can navigate one step backward in the stack:

```
this.props.navigation.goBack();
```

Let's modify the `<DeckScreen>` component so that tapping on a deck brings us to the `<ReviewScreen>`.

First, let's look at the `<Deck>` component, which is used by `<DeckScreen>` (see Example 10-16).

Example 10-16. src_checkpoint_01/components/DeckScreen/Deck.js

```
import React, { Component } from "react";
import { StyleSheet, View } from "react-native";

import DeckModel from "./../../data/Deck";
import Button from "./../Button";
import NormalText from "./../NormalText";
import colors from "./../../styles/colors";

class Deck extends Component {
  static displayName = "Deck";

  _review = () => {
    console.warn("Not implemented");
  };

  _addCards = () => {
    console.warn("Not implemented");
  };

  render() {
    return (
      <View style={styles.deckGroup}>

        <Button style={styles.deckButton} onPress={this._review}>
          <NormalText>
            {this.props.deck.name}: {this.props.count} cards
          </NormalText>
        </Button>

        <Button style={styles.editButton} onPress={this._addCards}>
          <NormalText>+</NormalText>
        </Button>
      </View>
    );
  }
}

const styles = StyleSheet.create({
  deckGroup: {
    flexDirection: "row",
    alignItems: "stretch",
    padding: 10,
    marginBottom: 5
  },
  deckButton: { backgroundColor: colors.pink, padding: 10, margin: 0, flex: 1 },
  editButton: {
    width: 60,
    backgroundColor: colors.pink2,
    justifyContent: "center",
    alignItems: "center",
```

```
    alignSelf: "center",
    padding: 0,
    paddingTop: 10,
    paddingBottom: 10,
    margin: 0,
    flex: 0
  }
});
```

```
export default Deck;
```

Let's modify _review() in *Deck.js* to invoke a review prop:

```
_review = () => {
  this.props.review();
}
```

Now this prop will be invoked when someone taps the button associated with a deck.

Next, we need to update *DeckScreen/index.js*.

Let's add a _review function here as well:

```
_review = () => {
  console.warn("Actual reviews not implemented");
  this.props.navigation.navigate("Review");
}
```

Note that we use the fat-arrow function declaration syntax in order to properly bind the function to the component class. While React lifecycle methods are automatically bound to the component instance, other methods are not.

Then, update the rendered <Deck> component to include the appropriate prop:

```
_mkDeckViews() {
  if (!this.state.decks) {
    return null;
  }

  return this.state.decks.map((deck) => {
    return (
      <Deck
        deck={deck}
        count={deck.cards.length}
        key={deck.id}
        review={this._review} />);
  });
}
```

Run the application. When you tap on a deck, it should bring you to the review screen. Nice!

Configuring the Header with navigationOptions

We can also pass in navigationOptions to the StackNavigator in order to configure what gets rendered in the header.

Let's update the *Flashcards.js* file to set some basic header style options (see Example 10-17).

Example 10-17. src_checkpoint_02/components/Flashcards.js

```
import React, { Component } from "react";
import { StyleSheet, View } from "react-native";
import { StackNavigator } from "react-navigation";

import Logo from "./Header/Logo";
import DeckScreen from "./DeckScreen";
import NewCardScreen from "./NewCardScreen";
import ReviewScreen from "./ReviewScreen";

let headerOptions = {
  headerStyle: { backgroundColor: "#FFFFFF" },
  headerLeft: <Logo />
};

let navigator = StackNavigator({
  Home: { screen: DeckScreen, navigationOptions: headerOptions },
  Review: { screen: ReviewScreen, navigationOptions: headerOptions },
  CardCreation: { screen: NewCardScreen, navigationOptions: headerOptions }
});

export default navigator;
```

Additionally, in the *DeckScreen/index.js* file, let's set some more navigationOptions.

```
    class DecksScreen extends Component {

      static navigationOptions = {
        title: 'All Decks'
      };


      ...
    }
```

Setting a title will change the rendered title in the StackNavigator header.

If we look at our application again, we can see the changes take effect (Figure 10-6).

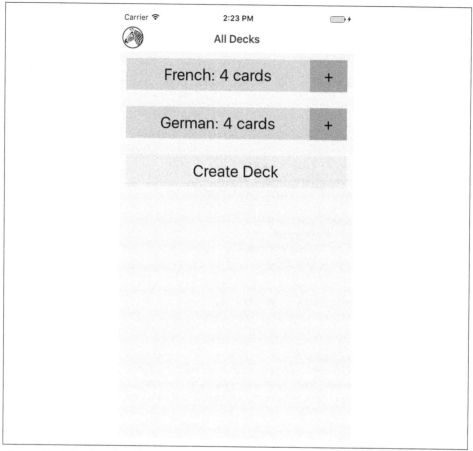

Figure 10-6. Setting the title via navigationOptions

Implementing the Rest

Now that we have the StackNavigator in place, we need to wire it up to the rest of the application. Specifically, the following interactions should work:

- Tapping a deck from the <DeckScreen> should navigate to the <ReviewScreen>
- Tapping the plus button from the <DeckScreen> should navigate to the <New CardScreen>
- Tapping Done from the <NewCardScreen> should navigate back to the <DeckScreen>
- Tapping Create Card from the <NewCardScreen> should navigate to a fresh <New CardScreen>

- Tapping Review Deck from the `<NewCardScreen>` should navigate to the `<ReviewScreen>`

- Tapping Stop Reviewing from the `<ReviewScreen>` should navigate back to the `<DeckScreen>`

- Tapping Done from the `<ReviewScreen>` should navigate back to the `<DeckScreen>`

- Creating a deck from the `<DeckScreen>` should navigate to the `<NewCardScreen>`

The updated code for this section is located on GitHub (*https://github.com/bonniee/learning-react-native/tree/2.0.0/src/flashcards/src_checkpoint_02*). The following files will be updated:

- *components/DeckScreen/Deck.js*
- *components/DeckScreen/DeckCreation.js*
- *components/DeckScreen/index.js*
- *components/NewCardScreen/index.js*
- *components/ReviewScreen/index.js*
- *components/Flashcards.js*
- *components/Header/Logo.js*

Summary

Organizing larger applications in React Native is sometimes a challenge. While we've looked at the pieces necessary to build React Native applications in previous chapters, the flashcards application is a meatier example of how it all fits together. By using the React Navigation library, we can combine many disparate screens of an app into a cohesive user experience.

In the next section, we'll improve upon the flashcards application by adding Redux, a state management library, and integrating it with `AsyncStorage` to persist state between application launches.

State Management in Larger Applications

In Chapter 10, we used the flashcard application as a jumping-off point to discuss the structure of larger applications. One of the common issues that React applications encounter as they grow is *state management*. React Native is no different: as our application gets larger, we can benefit from using a state management library. In this chapter, we'll look at Redux, a library for managing data flow, and integrate it with our flashcards application. We'll also integrate AsyncStorage with our Redux store.

Using Redux to Manage State

Redux is based somewhat on the Flux data flow pattern, as well as functional programming concepts. Previous examples we've looked at in this book haven't required much in the way of data flow management. With smaller applications, communicating between components is usually a trivial issue. Consider the case where a button tap has an impact on the parent's state:

```
class Child extends Component {
  render() {
    <TouchableOpacity onPress={this.props.onPress}>
      <Text>Child Component</Text>
    </TouchableOpacity>
  }
}
```

By passing a callback from the parent to the child, we can alert the parent about interactions with the child:

```
class Parent extends Component {
  constructor(props) {
    super(props);
    this.initialState = { numTaps: 0 };
  }
```

```
_handlePress = () => {
  this.setState({numTaps: this.state.numTaps + 1});
}

render() {
  <Child onPress={this._handlePress}/>
  }
}
```

For simple use cases, this pattern works just fine.

Our need for a more robust data flow architecture becomes apparent when we consider a more complex interaction. What happens when a component much farther down the component tree needs to impact an application state located on a higher level? It's very easy to end up with a tangle of spaghetti, and to spend tedious time stringing callbacks through your code. Managing active routes, handling user interactions, fetching data from the server, animating changes—as you add more state to your application, the complexity grows, and cascading updates can be triggered in unpredictable ways.

Redux is one of many libraries designed to make it easier to manage your application's state, with the goal of making state changes predictable and easy to manage.

In Redux, state is located in a single object, in a single *store*, which acts as the sole source of truth. Components that need to render based on state can *connect* to that store and receive the state as *props*. Components cannot modify state directly.

Changes to state are triggered by a set of predefined *actions*. A single *reducer* combines the previous state and information from the action in order to calculate the new state. Thus, logic about how your state can change, and when, is centralized in one easy-to-debug location.

All of this will likely make more sense in practice than in theory. Let's install Redux and look at how to add it to our flashcard application. In addition to the redux package, we will want to install the react-redux package, which contains the React bindings for redux.

```
npm install --save redux react-redux
```

Actions

First things first: let's define what types of *actions* can result in state changes. We're going to create some string constants to represent the different types of actions (see Example 11-1).

Example 11-1. src_checkpoint_03/actions/types.js

```
export const ADD_DECK = "ADD_DECK";
export const ADD_CARD = "ADD_CARD";
export const REVIEW_DECK = "REVIEW_DECK";
export const STOP_REVIEW = "STOP_REVIEW";
export const NEXT_REVIEW = "NEXT_REVIEW";
```

Each of these action types represents a user interaction and covers the basic functionality of our application: adding cards or decks, or starting or stopping a review.

An *action* in Redux is an object that contains a key named *type*, and some optional extra data. We need to add some *action creators* to create these objects (see Example 11-2). While we could theoretically skip having a separate file with action creators, centralizing this code will help keep our React components clean, and gives us a single file to glance at to find action definitions.

Example 11-2. src_checkpoint_03/actions/creators.js

```
import {
  ADD_DECK,
  ADD_CARD,
  REVIEW_DECK,
  STOP_REVIEW,
  NEXT_REVIEW
} from "./types";

import Card from "../data/Card";
import Deck from "../data/Deck";

export const addDeck = name => {
  return { type: ADD_DECK, data: new Deck(name) };
};

export const addCard = (front, back, deckID) => {
  return { type: ADD_CARD, data: new Card(front, back, deckID) };
};

export const reviewDeck = deckID => {
  return { type: REVIEW_DECK, data: { deckID: deckID } };
};

export const stopReview = () => {
  return { type: STOP_REVIEW, data: {} };
};

export const nextReview = () => {
  return { type: NEXT_REVIEW, data: {} };
};
```

In many ways, these action creators act as convenience functions. For example, the addDeck action creator takes a deck name as a parameter and then handles the actual construction of a Deck.

Reducers

Actions represent things that happened in your application. *Reducers* describe how your application state changes in response to actions. A reducer is a "pure function": it has no side effects, and its return value is determined only by its inputs. (Don't call Math.random in a reducer.)

The simplest reducer we could write would look like:

```
const reducer = (state = {}, action) => {
  return state;
}
```

Our state is going to contain two items: an array of decks and information about the current review. The default state will look like this:

```
decks: [],
currentReview: {
  deckID = null,
  questions = [],
  currentQuestionIndex = 0
}
```

Let's start writing our first reducer by looking at the ADD_DECK action. Looking back at *actions/creators.js*, we see the following action:

```
{
  type: ADD_DECK,
  data: new Deck(name)
}
```

If we want to write a reducer for the decks key, the signature needs to look like:

```
const decksReducer = (state = [], action) => {
  // returns some state
}
```

We want to add the new deck from our action to the existing state, so let's implement the deckReducer.

```
const deckReducer = (state = [], action) => {
  switch (action.type) {
    case ADD_DECK:
      return state.concat(action.data);
  }
  return state;
}
```

First, we need a `switch` statement based on the action's type. We're only handling the `ADD_DECK` action for now. In all other cases we return the original state, unmodified. This is very important—don't forget to handle the default case!

Then, if the action type is in fact `ADD_DECK`, we concatenate the new deck to our existing deck state and return it.

Now let's implement the rest of the `deckReducer` (see Example 11-3).

Example 11-3. src_checkpoint_03/reducers/decks.js

```
import { ADD_DECK, ADD_CARD } from "../actions/types";

function decksWithNewCard(oldDecks, card) {
  return oldDecks.map(deck => {
    if (deck.id === card.deckID) {
      deck.addCard(card);
      return deck;
    } else {
      return deck;
    }
  });
}

const reducer = (state = [], action) => {
  console.warn("Changes are not persisted to disk");

  switch (action.type) {
    case ADD_DECK:
      return state.concat(action.data);
    case ADD_CARD:
      return decksWithNewCard(state, action.data);
  }
  return state;
};

export default reducer;
```

Next, let's look at the reviews reducer (Example 11-4). This reducer will handle the `REVIEW_DECK`, `NEXT_REVIEW`, and `STOP_REVIEW` actions. Handling `STOP_REVIEW` is simplest: we'll replace the state with the default state. For `NEXT_REVIEW`, we increment the review index. Handling `REVIEW_DECK` is somewhat more complex because we have to take a deck of cards and generate questions based on it.

Example 11-4. src_checkpoint_03/reducers/reviews.js

```
import { mkReviews } from "./../data/QuizCardView";
import { REVIEW_DECK, NEXT_REVIEW, STOP_REVIEW } from "./../actions/types";
```

```
export const mkReviewState = (
  deckID = null,
  questions = [],
  currentQuestionIndex = 0
) => {
  return { deckID, questions, currentQuestionIndex };
};

function findDeck(decks, id) {
  return decks.find(d => {
    return d.id === id;
  });
}

function generateReviews(deck) {
  return mkReviewState(deck.id, mkReviews(deck.cards), 0);
}

function nextReview(state) {
  return mkReviewState(
    state.deckID,
    state.questions,
    state.currentQuestionIndex + 1
  );
}

const reducer = (state = mkReviewstate(), action, decks) => {
  switch (action.type) {
    case REVIEW_DECK:
      return generateReviews(findDeck(decks, action.data.deckID));
    case NEXT_REVIEW:
      return nextReview(state);
    case STOP_REVIEW:
      return mkReviewState();
  }
  return state;
};

export default reducer;
```

Note that this reducer depends on deck information, so its signature is slightly different than the decksReducer.

Now let's wire them up together. In Redux, you only connect a single reducer to your store, so we need to combine these into one reducer (see Example 11-5).

Example 11-5. src_checkpoint_03/reducers/index.js

```
import { MockDecks, MockCards } from "././../data/Mocks";

import DecksReducer from "./decks";
```

```
import ReviewReducer, { mkReviewState } from "./reviews";

const initialState = () => {
  return { decks: MockDecks, currentReview: mkReviewState() };
};

export const reducer = (state = initialState(), action) => {
  let decks = DecksReducer(state.decks, action);

  return {
    decks: decks,
    currentReview: ReviewReducer(state.currentReview, action, decks)
  };
};
```

Now that we've written some Redux-specific code, the next step is to integrate it into our actual application.

Connecting Redux

Remember how we said that state is located in a single Redux *store*? Let's open up *components/Flashcard.js*, which is the root component for our application, and create that store.

First we need to import the createStore method from redux, as well as the reducer that we just created in *reducers/index.js*. Then we can create the store.

```
import { createStore } from "redux";
import { reducer } from "../reducers/index";

let store = createStore(reducer);
```

Next, in order to use this store from our application, we need to add a <Provider> component.

Wrapping your application's root component in a <Provider> makes the Redux store available to any component at any part of the component hierarchy. Remember, state in Redux is read-only, so there's no risk of complications from *reading* state at any point in the component hierarchy. <Provider> is part of the react-redux package.

Let's wire that in. Example 11-6 shows the full component file after we integrate our Redux store.

Example 11-6. src_checkpoint_03/components/Flashcards.js

```
import React, { Component } from "react";
import { StyleSheet, View } from "react-native";
import { StackNavigator } from "react-navigation";
import { createStore } from "redux";
```

```
import { Provider } from "react-redux";

import { reducer } from "../reducers/index";

import Logo from "./Header/Logo";
import DeckScreen from "./DeckScreen";
import NewCardScreen from "./NewCardScreen";
import ReviewScreen from "./ReviewScreen";

let store = createStore(reducer);

let headerOptions = {
  headerStyle: { backgroundColor: "#FFFFFF" },
  headerLeft: <Logo />
};

const Navigator = StackNavigator({
  Home: { screen: DeckScreen, navigationOptions: headerOptions },
  Review: { screen: ReviewScreen, navigationOptions: headerOptions },
  CardCreation: {
    screen: NewCardScreen,
    path: "createCard/:deckID",
    navigationOptions: headerOptions
  }
});

class App extends Component {
  render() {
    return (
      <Provider store={store}>
        <Navigator />
      </Provider>
    );
  }
}

export default App;
```

Now that we've integrated Redux, let's use it to render some data. We'll start by modifying the <DecksScreen> component to display decks based on the contents of the Redux store.

In order to *connect* a given component to our Redux store, we use the react-redux bindings.

```
import { connect } from "react-redux"
```

Then we need to define two functions: mapStateToProps and mapDispatchToProps.

mapStateToProps describes how the Redux store's state will be provided to this component as props. Our state includes an array of decks. We'll want to calculate the counts here, too.

```
const mapStateToProps = state => {
  return {
    decks: state.decks,
    counts: state.decks.reduce(
      (sum, deck) => {
        sum[deck.id] = deck.cards.length;
        return sum;
      },
      {}
    )
  };
};
```

Meanwhile, `mapDispatchToProps` defines the props that a component will receive, which can be used to dispatch actions. We need to import our action creators and then invoke them from here.

```
import { addDeck, reviewDeck } from "./../../actions/creators";
...
const mapDispatchToProps = dispatch => {
  return {
    createDeck: deckAction => {
      dispatch(deckAction);
    },
    reviewDeck: deckID => {
      dispatch(reviewDeck(deckID));
    }
  };
};
```

Finally, we need to call `connect()` to create a Redux-connected component.

```
export default connect(mapStateToProps, mapDispatchToProps)(DecksScreen);
```

Pulling it all together, we can use these new props (`reviewDeck`, `createDeck`, `decks`, and `counts`) in our component. Now, the `<DecksScreen>` will render based on props received from Redux, and it will also dispatch Redux actions instead of modifying state directly (see Example 11-7).

Example 11-7. src_checkpoint_03/components/DeckScreen/index.js

```
import React, { Component } from "react";
import { View } from "react-native";

import { connect } from "react-redux";

import { MockDecks } from "./../../data/Mocks";
import { addDeck, reviewDeck } from "./../../actions/creators";
import Deck from "./Deck";
import DeckCreation from "./DeckCreation";

class DecksScreen extends Component {
```

```
    static displayName = "DecksScreen";

    static navigationOptions = { title: "All Decks" };

    _createDeck = name => {
      let createDeckAction = addDeck(name);
      this.props.createDeck(createDeckAction);
      this.props.navigation.navigate("CardCreation", {
        deckID: createDeckAction.data.id
      });
    };

    _addCards = deckID => {
      this.props.navigation.navigate("CardCreation", { deckID: deckID });
    };

    _review = deckID => {
      this.props.reviewDeck(deckID);
      this.props.navigation.navigate("Review");
    };

    _mkDeckViews() {
      if (!this.props.decks) {
        return null;
      }

      return this.props.decks.map(deck => {
        return (
          <Deck
            deck={deck}
            count={this.props.counts[deck.id]}
            key={deck.id}
            add={() => {
              this._addCards(deck.id);
            }}
            review={() => {
              this._review(deck.id);
            }}
          />
        );
      });
    }

  render() {
    return (
      <View>
        {this._mkDeckViews()}
        <DeckCreation create={this._createDeck} />
      </View>
    );
  }
}
```

```
const mapDispatchToProps = dispatch => {
  return {
    createDeck: deckAction => {
      dispatch(deckAction);
    },
    reviewDeck: deckID => {
      dispatch(reviewDeck(deckID));
    }
  };
};

const mapStateToProps = state => {
  return {
    decks: state.decks,
    counts: state.decks.reduce(
      (sum, deck) => {
        sum[deck.id] = deck.cards.length;
        return sum;
      },
      {}
    )
  };
};

export default connect(mapStateToProps, mapDispatchToProps)(DecksScreen);
```

In general, when you are converting to Redux or a similar library, replacing access to or mutating this.state is a common pattern. The more your components rely on props instead of state, the easier it is to manage growing complexity in your application.

We need to make similar updates to the <NewCardScreen> and <ReviewScreen> components as well; see Examples 11-8 and 11-9, respectively. As we did with <DecksScreen>, we implement mapDispatchToProps and mapStateToProps for each of them.

Example 11-8. src_checkpoint_03/components/NewCardScreen/index.js

```
import React, { Component } from "react";
import { StyleSheet, View } from "react-native";

import DeckModel from "./../../data/Deck";
import { addCard } from "./../../actions/creators";
import { connect } from "react-redux";

import Button from "../Button";
import LabeledInput from "../LabeledInput";
import NormalText from "../NormalText";
import colors from "./../../styles/colors";
```

```
class NewCard extends Component {
  static navigationOptions = { title: "Create Card" };

  static initialState = { front: "", back: "" };

  constructor(props) {
    super(props);
    this.state = this.initialState;
  }

  _deckID = () => {
    return this.props.navigation.state.params.deckID;
  };

  _handleFront = text => {
    this.setState({ front: text });
  };

  _handleBack = text => {
    this.setState({ back: text });
  };

  _createCard = () => {
    this.props.createCard(this.state.front, this.state.back, this._deckID());
    this.props.navigation.navigate("CardCreation", { deckID: this._deckID() });
  };

  _reviewDeck = () => {
    this.props.navigation.navigate("Review");
  };

  _doneCreating = () => {
    this.props.navigation.navigate("Home");
  };

  render() {
    return (
      <View>
        <LabeledInput
          label="Front"
          clearOnSubmit={false}
          onEntry={this._handleFront}
          onChange={this._handleFront}
        />
        <LabeledInput
          label="Back"
          clearOnSubmit={false}
          onEntry={this._handleBack}
          onChange={this._handleBack}
        />
```

```
              <Button style={styles.createButton} onPress={this._createCard}>
                <NormalText>Create Card</NormalText>
              </Button>

              <View style={styles.buttonRow}>
                <Button style={styles.secondaryButton} onPress={this._doneCreating}>
                  <NormalText>Done</NormalText>
                </Button>

                <Button style={styles.secondaryButton} onPress={this._reviewDeck}>
                  <NormalText>Review Deck</NormalText>
                </Button>
              </View>
            </View>
          );
        }
      }

      const styles = StyleSheet.create({
        createButton: { backgroundColor: colors.green },
        secondaryButton: { backgroundColor: colors.blue },
        buttonRow: { flexDirection: "row" }
      });

      const mapStateToProps = state => {
        return { decks: state.decks };
      };

      const mapDispatchToProps = dispatch => {
        return {
          createCard: (front, back, deckID) => {
            dispatch(addCard(front, back, deckID));
          }
        };
      };

      export default connect(mapStateToProps, mapDispatchToProps)(NewCard);
```

Example 11-9. src_checkpoint_03/components/ReviewScreen/index.js

```
import React, { Component } from "react";
import { StyleSheet, View } from "react-native";

import { connect } from "react-redux";
import ViewCard from "./ViewCard";
import { mkReviewSummary } from "./ReviewSummary";
import colors from "./../../styles/colors";
import { reviewCard, nextReview, stopReview } from "./../../actions/creators";

class ReviewScreen extends Component {
  static displayName = "ReviewScreen";
```

```
static navigationOptions = { title: "Review" };

constructor(props) {
  super(props);
  this.state = { numReviewed: 0, numCorrect: 0 };
}

onReview = correct => {
  if (correct) {
    this.setState({ numCorrect: this.state.numCorrect + 1 });
  }
  this.setState({ numReviewed: this.state.numReviewed + 1 });
};

_nextReview = () => {
  this.props.nextReview();
};

_quitReviewing = () => {
  this.props.stopReview();
  this.props.navigation.goBack();
};

_contents() {
  if (!this.props.reviews || this.props.reviews.length === 0) {
    return null;
  }

  if (this.props.currentReview < this.props.reviews.length) {
    return (
      <ViewCard
        onReview={this.onReview}
        continue={this._nextReview}
        quit={this._quitReviewing}
        {...this.props.reviews[this.props.currentReview]}
      />
    );
  } else {
    let percent = this.state.numCorrect / this.state.numReviewed;
    return mkReviewSummary(percent, this._quitReviewing);
  }
}

render() {
  return (
    <View style={styles.container}>
      {this._contents()}
    </View>
  );
}
}
```

```
const styles = StyleSheet.create({
  container: { backgroundColor: colors.blue, flex: 1, paddingTop: 24 }
});

const mapDispatchToProps = dispatch => {
  return {
    nextReview: () => {
      dispatch(nextReview());
    },
    stopReview: () => {
      dispatch(stopReview());
    }
  };
};

const mapStateToProps = state => {
  return {
    reviews: state.currentReview.questions,
    currentReview: state.currentReview.currentQuestionIndex
  };
};

export default connect(mapStateToProps, mapDispatchToProps)(ReviewScreen);
```

Persisting Data with AsyncStorage

Right now, our flashcard application's state isn't persisted, so if we add new decks or cards and then restart the app, our data is lost. Let's fix this by saving the application's state with AsyncStorage.

This is an example of how Redux can really shine: because our state management logic is centralized, making this change is simpler than it would otherwise be.

We'll start by adding a file that handles read/write logic for persisting our state to disk; see Example 11-10. Remember, AsyncStorage.getItem and AsyncStorage.setItem are both asynchronous APIs.

Example 11-10. src_checkpoint_04/storage/decks.js

```
import { AsyncStorage } from "react-native";
import Deck from "./../data/Deck";
export const DECK_KEY = "flashcards:decks";
import { MockDecks } from "./../data/Mocks";

async function read(key, deserializer) {
  try {
    let val = await AsyncStorage.getItem(key);
    if (val !== null) {
      let readValue = JSON.parse(val).map(serialized => {
        return deserializer(serialized);
```

```
      });
      return readValue;
    } else {
      console.info(`${key} not found on disk.`);
      return [];
    }
  } catch (error) {
    console.warn("AsyncStorage error: ", error.message);
  }
}

async function write(key, item) {
  try {
    await AsyncStorage.setItem(key, JSON.stringify(item));
  } catch (error) {
    console.error("AsyncStorage error: ", error.message);
  }
}

export const readDecks = () => {
  return read(DECK_KEY, Deck.fromObject);
};

export const writeDecks = decks => {
  return write(DECK_KEY, decks);
};

// For debug/test purposes.
const replaceData = writeDecks(MockDecks);
```

Remember that our Redux state has two elements: decks and currentReview.
Because currentReview is transient information, we only need to worry about saving
decks.

Now that we have an easy way of reading and writing our decks to AsyncStorage, let's
add a new action type, LOAD_DATA, to *actions/types.js*, as shown in Example 11-11.

Example 11-11. Adding a new type to src_checkpoint_04/actions/types.js

```
export const LOAD_DATA = "LOAD_DATA";
```

We also need an accompanying action creator in *actions/creators.js* (see
Example 11-12).

Example 11-12. Adding a new action creator to src_checkpoint_04/actions/creators.js

```
export const loadData = data => {
  return { type: LOAD_DATA, data: data };
};
```

Next, update *Flashcards.js* to load data from disk after our store is created.

```
import { readDecks } from "../storage/decks";
import { loadData } from "../actions/creators";

...

let store = createStore(reducer);

// On application start, read saved state from disk.
readDecks().then(decks => {
  store.dispatch(loadData(decks));
});
```

Now that we have dispatched the action, we need to update our deck reducer to handle the LOAD_DATA action. Additionally, when handling the ADD_CARD or ADD_DECK actions, this reducer should save the deck state (see Example 11-13).

Example 11-13. Updating src_checkpoint_04/reducers/decks.js to save state

```
import { ADD_DECK, ADD_CARD, LOAD_DATA } from "../actions/types";
import Deck from "./../data/Deck";
import { writeDecks } from "./../storage/decks";

function decksWithNewCard(oldDecks, card) {
  let newState = oldDecks.map(deck => {
    if (deck.id === card.deckID) {
      deck.addCard(card);
      return deck;
    } else {
      return deck;
    }
  });
  saveDecks(newState);
  return newState;
}

function saveDecks(state) {
  writeDecks(state);
  return state;
}

const reducer = (state = [], action) => {
  switch (action.type) {
    case LOAD_DATA:
      return action.data;
    case ADD_DECK:
      let newState = state.concat(action.data);
      saveDecks(newState);
      return newState;
    case ADD_CARD:
```

```
    return decksWithNewCard(state, action.data);

  }
  return state;
};

export default reducer;
```

And...that's it! Because state is managed by Redux, we can be confident that by modifying our deck reducer, we've ensured that all relevant state changes will be persisted to AsyncStorage.

Summary and Homework

A common critique of Redux—and similar state management libraries—is that it adds significant boilerplate to your application. Indeed, we had to write several new files in order to integrate Redux into our flashcard application. However, by expressing state relationships explicitly rather than mutating state locally, this "boilerplate" makes existing complexity much more manageable. It's harder to write state-based bugs with Redux! You also get some nice bonuses like time travel debugging. Plus, as we saw when integrating AsyncStorage, making further changes to your application becomes much easier.

Which particular state management library you use doesn't matter so much; there are many reasonable ways to structure a large application. However, as with any large React application, if you don't plan for state management, eventually you will probably start to encounter bugs related to state mutations and have difficulty making changes to existing components. This is a good sign that you need to put more planning into your state and data flow management.

The flashcard application is meant to serve as a reference. In many ways, it's a "minimum viable project," and there are plenty of ways it could be improved. That being said, there's still plenty to explore in the codebase, and I encourage you to dig into it.

If you want to get some more practice working within the context of React Native, check out the GitHub repository and try extending the flashcard application. Here are some ideas to get you started:

- Add the ability to delete decks
- Add a screen where you can view all cards in a deck
- Display statistics about review performance over time
- Experiment with different styles

Conclusion

If you've made it this far, congratulations!

We've gone from creating your very first "Hello, World" React Native application all the way up through a complex, fully featured application with total code reuse across iOS and Android. In order to do so, we started by looking at the basic components for React Native, and how to style them. We learned how to work with touch and platform native APIs, like the AsyncStorage and Geolocation APIs. We covered how to debug React Native applications with the developer tools, and how to deploy your applications to real devices. For functionality beyond the standard React Native library, we also saw how to use native Objective-C and Java modules as well as third-party JavaScript libraries using npm.

Your knowledge of JavaScript and React, coupled with the topics we've covered in this book, should enable you to quickly and efficiently write cross-platform mobile applications for Android and iOS. Of course, there's still plenty to learn, and this single book can't cover *all* the things you'll need to know in order to develop mobile applications with React Native. If you get stuck or have questions, reach out to the community, whether that's on Stack Overflow (*http://stackoverflow.com/questions/tagged/react-native*) or on IRC (*irc.lc/freenode/reactnative*).

Keep in touch! Join the *Learning React Native* mailing list at LearningReactNative.com for more resources and updates related to the book. You can also find me on Twitter as @brindelle (*http://twitter.com/brindelle*).

Finally, and most importantly, have fun! I'm looking forward to seeing what you build.

Modern JavaScript Syntax

Some of the code samples in this book use modern JavaScript syntax. If you're not familiar with this syntax, don't worry—it's a pretty straightforward translation from the JavaScript you might be accustomed to.

ECMAScript 5, or ES5, is the JavaScript language specification with the broadest adoption. However, there are many compelling language features introduced in ES6, ES7, and beyond. React Native uses Babel (*https://babeljs.io/*), the JavaScript compiler, to transform our JavaScript and JSX code. One of Babel's features is its ability to compile newer-style syntax into ES5-compliant JavaScript. This enables us to use language features from ES6 and beyond throughout our React codebase.

let and const

In pre-ES6 JavaScript, we use var to declare variables.

In ES6, there are two additional ways to declare variables: let and const. A variable declared with const cannot be reassigned; that is to say, the following is invalid:

```
const count = 2;
count = count + 1; // BAD
```

Variables declared with let or var may be reassigned. A variable declared with let may only be used in the same block as it is defined.

Some of the examples in this book still use var, but you'll also see let and const. Don't worry about the distinctions too much.

Importing Modules

We could use CommonJS module syntax to export our components and other Java-Script modules (Example A-1). In this system, we use `require` to import other modules, and assign a value to `module.exports` in order to make a file's contents available to other modules.

Example A-1. Requiring and exporting modules using CommonJS syntax

```
var OtherComponent = require('./other_component');

class MyComponent extends Component {
  ...
}

module.exports = MyComponent;
```

With ES6 module syntax (*http://mzl.la/21cv5QF*), we can use the `export` and `import` commands instead. Example A-2 shows the equivalent code, using ES6 module syntax.

Example A-2. Importing and exporting modules using ES6 module syntax

```
import OtherComponent from './other_component';

class MyComponent extends Component {
  ...
}

export default MyComponent;
```

Destructuring

Destructuring assignments (*http://mzl.la/1I6ppBl*) provide us with a convenient shorthand for extracting data from objects.

Take this ES5-compliant snippet:

```
var myObj = {a: 1, b: 2};
var a = myObj.a;
var b = myObj.b;
```

We can use destructuring to do this more succinctly:

```
var {a, b} = {a: 1, b: 2};
```

You'll often see this used with `import` statements. When we `import` React, we're actually receiving an object. We *could* import without using destructuring, as shown in Example A-3.

Example A-3. Importing the Component class without destructuring

```
import React from "react";
let Component = React.Component;
```

But it's much nicer to use destructuring, as shown in Example A-4.

Example A-4. Using destructuring to import the Component class

```
import React, { Component } from "react";
```

Function Shorthand

ES6's function shorthand (*http://mzl.la/1SW4AJ4*) is also convenient. In ES5-compliant JavaScript, we define functions as shown in Example A-5.

Example A-5. Longhand function declaration

```
render: function() {
  return <Text>Hi</Text>;
}
```

Writing out `function` over and over again can get annoying. Example A-6 shows the same function, this time applying ES6's function shorthand.

Example A-6. Shorthand function declaration

```
render() {
  return <Text>Hi</Text>;
}
```

Fat-Arrow Functions

In ES5-compliant JavaScript, we often need to `bind` our functions to make sure that their context (i.e., the value of `this`) is as expected (Example A-7). This is especially common when we're dealing with callbacks.

Example A-7. Binding functions manually with ES5-compliant JavaScript

```
var callbackFunc = function(val) {
  console.log('Do something');
}.bind(this);
```

Fat-arrow functions (*http://mzl.la/1MN2cRj*) are automatically bound so we don't need to do that ourselves (Example A-8).

Example A-8. Using a fat-arrow function for binding

```
var callbackFunc = (val) => {
  console.log('Do something');
};
```

Default Parameters

You can specify default parameters for a function, as shown in Example A-9.

Example A-9. Using default parameters

```
var helloWorld = (name = "Bonnie") => {
      console.log("Hello, " + name);
}

helloWorld("Zach"); // Prints "Hello, Zach"
helloWorld(); // Prints "Hello, Bonnie"
```

This syntax is convenient when you want to guarantee a sensible default value for a parameter.

String Interpolation

In ES5-compliant JavaScript, we might build a string by using code such as that in Example A-10.

Example A-10. String concatenation in ES5-compliant JavaScript

```
var API_KEY = 'abcdefg';
var url = 'http://someapi.com/request&key=' + API_KEY;
```

Instead, we can use tempate strings (*http://mzl.la/21cvceS*), which support multiline strings and string interpolation. By enclosing a string in backticks, we can insert other variable values using the ${} syntax (Example A-11).

Example A-11. String interpolation in ES6

```
var API_KEY = 'abcdefg';
var url = `http://someapi.com/request&key=${API_KEY}`;
```

Working with Promises

A promise is an object representing something that will eventually happen. Instead of handcrafting your handling of success and error callbacks, promises have a consistent API for interacting with asynchronous operations.

Let's say that you have two callbacks: one for success and one for error handling (see Example A-12).

Example A-12. Defining two callbacks

```
function successCallback(result) {
  console.log("It succeeded: ", result);
}

function errorCallback(error) {
  console.log("It failed: ", error);
}
```

An old-style function might expect two callbacks and call one of them based on success or failure (see Example A-13).

Example A-13. Passing success and error callbacks in old-style JavaScript

```
uploadToSomeAPI(successCallback, errorCallback);
```

With modern promise-based syntax, you can pass success and error callbacks as shown in Example A-14.

Example A-14. Passing success and error callbacks with promises

```
uploadToSomeAPI().then(successCallback, errorCallback);
```

These two examples look very similar, but the advantages of using promises becomes evident when you have many callbacks or asynchronous operations to execute. Let's say that you need to upload some data to an API, update a user interface, and then look for new data.

With old-style callbacks, we can quickly end up in what is sometimes referred to as "callback hell" (Example A-15).

Example A-15. Chaining callbacks together can get messy quickly and is also repetitive

```
uploadToSomeAPI(
  (result) => {
    updateUserInterface(
      result,
      uiUpdateResult => {
        checkForNewData(
          uiUpdateResult,
          newDataResult => {
            successCallback(newDataResult);
          },
          errorCallback
        );
      },
      errorCallback
    );
  }, errorCallback
);
```

With promises, we can chain calls to the then method, as Example A-16 shows.

Example A-16. Chaining promises together is simpler

```
uploadToSomeAPI()
  .then(result => updateUserInterface(result))
  .then(uiUpdateResult => checkForNewData(uiUpdateResult))
  .then(newDataResult => successCallback(newDataResult))
  .catch(errorCallback)
```

This keeps our code cleaner. It also means that we don't need to reimplement callback handling each time we write a function.

Deploying Your Application

Once you have built your *totally awesome* application, you'll want to get it into the hands of your users.

The process for building and deploying your production application varies by platform, and both Google and Apple periodically update the specific steps required. However, the basic process remains the same:

1. Triple-check your assets: application icon, launch screen, and so on.
2. Specify target OS versions and devices.
3. Create a release build.
4. Get your paperwork in order.
5. Create an App Store and Play Store listing, including promotional screenshots.
6. Send the app to your beta testers and solicit feedback.
7. Submit for review.
8. Release!

Check Your Application Assets and Specify Target OS Versions and Devices

It's easy to overlook these steps during development. You'll want to make sure that you have a suitable application icon and launch screen for your application in the correct sizes and resolutions for all the devices you intend to target.

Similarly, for any images, video, or other assets utilized by your application, make sure that you have included versions appropriate to each targeted device.

Create a Release Build

You will need to compile your application into a production-ready release build before shipping it off to your end users. This version of your application won't have debugging enabled and will include the bundled JavaScript instead of relying on the React Native packager.

For both iOS and Android, the official React Native documentation (*https://facebook.github.io/react-native/docs/running-on-device.html*) includes guidance on creating production-ready builds.

Complete Your Paperwork

In order to distribute your application to Android devices, you'll probably want to register with Google Play (*https://developer.android.com*). Similarly, you'll need to register for an Apple Developer account (*https://developer.apple.com*) in order to submit to the App Store.

As part of this process, you need to provide some standard information, such as contact and payment information.

Beta Test Your Application

You'll want to test your application on a variety of devices and operating system versions. How does it perform in landscape versus portrait mode? With low battery? With a slow network? What happens when you get interrupted by push notifications?

Getting your application into the hands of real users is the best way to evaluate how your application performs in real-world scenarios. Both the Play Store and the App Store have built-in programs to facilitate distribution of your application to beta testers.

Create a Listing

You'll need to convince people to download your application! Gather your promotional screenshots, select the appropriate category, and write a compelling description.

Once that's done, you can submit your application for review.

Wait for Review

As web developers, we're used to having more control over our deploy processes. You may be accustomed to shipping code to production many times in a single day, where versions are usually a nonissue. With the iOS App Store and Google Play Store, deployment is more complicated, and new version releases typically require review. Review times vary from a day to a couple of weeks. Thus, it's important to take the submission and review process into account during your planning phase.

Release

After putting in the hard work to create your application, seeing it go live (Figure B-1) can feel exhilarating. However, releasing your application to users is just the beginning, as you'll have to support your application postrelease. Unlike the web, where you can deploy often and easily, new mobile versions take time, and have a longer lifespan. Many iOS and Android users don't have auto-updating enabled, so every version counts. And at minimum you'll need to wait for application review each time you wish to submit an update or bug fix. (For truly critical bug fixes, you can request an expedited review, but use these carefully.)

Figure B-1. The flashcard application, live on the Play Store

And, finally: congratulations on shipping your app!

Working with Expo Applications

Expo is a tool that allows you to write React Native apps without using Xcode or Android Studio. Projects created with the Create React Native App tool are Expo projects.

Expo makes it very easy to develop on your physical device and removes many of the initial roadblocks to getting started with React Native. Thus, it's a great choice while you're learning to develop using React Native.

You can read more about Expo and install the Expo mobile app at expo.io (*https://expo.io/*).

Ejecting from Expo

Any project that relies on custom native code (either your own, or third-party modules that instruct you to run `react-native link` to install them) will not work with Expo. Expo provides a way to "eject" from Expo into a traditional, full React Native project. Ejecting will create a full React Native project from your existing Expo application. This is a one-way migration, so you won't be able to go back to Expo afterwards.

You will also need to eject from Expo if you want more control over building and publishing your application for the iOS App Store or Google Play Store.

More information is available in the Create React Native App documentation (*https://github.com/react-community/create-react-native-app*).

Index

Symbols

symbol, 117

A

absolute positioning, 84-85 (see also layouts)
acknowledgments, xiii
Android
    <Drawer LayoutAndroid>, 70
    <ToolbarAndroid>, 70, 133
    Android-only components, 133
    creating applications for, 14, 16
    debugging application problems, 152
        (see also debugging and developer tools)
    deployment and release steps, 215-217
    design guidelines, 71
    failure to boot virtual device, 152
    human interface guidelines, 137
    previewing your app on, 15
    react-native-video component, 127-130
    rendering images on, 42
    running apps on, 18
    running apps on simulators, 25, 88, 94, 155
    View, 8
    viewing logs, 142
    writing Java native modules for, 124-127
Android Studio, 18
animations, 50
applications, building
    environment setup choices, 13
    environment setup using Create React
        Native App command, 14-16
    environment setup using traditional
        approach, 16-18
    exploring sample code, 19-22
    weather app example, 22-36
applications, building larger
    Flashcard application example, 163-166
    project structure, 166-181
    state management, 189-206
    using React Navigation, 181-187
applications, deploying, 215-217
assets
    checking before deployment, 215
    sizing appropriately, 152
AsyncStorage API, 103, 203-206
attributions, xi
auto-updating, 217

B

Babel compiler, 209
background images, adding, 32, 110
beta testing, 216
bridge interface, 7, 12
<Button> component, 44, 108, 173

C

CameraRoll API
    getPhotoParams, 100
    interacting with, 99
    rendering images from, 101
    requesting images, 100
    uploading images to servers, 102
Chrome Developer Tools, 139, 142
code examples, obtaining and using, xi
code signing, configuring, 17
components
    binding callbacks to, 25
    changing callbacks on, 30

M

MDN Geolocation API web specification, 91
modules and native code
    benefits of modular approach, 74
    cross-platform native modules, 130
    definition of native modules, 117
    importing JavaScript, 210
    importing modules, 21
    installing JavaScript libraries, 113
    installing third-party, 115
    Java native modules, 124-130
    Objective-C modules, 116-124
    use cases for, 130
MP4 video assets, 116

N

native code (see modules and native code)
navigation
    adding react-navigation to project, 182
    components for, 69
    configuring headers, 185
    creating a StackNavigator, 182
    implementing interactions, 186
    transitioning between scenes, 182
<Navigator> component, 69
<NavigatorIOS> component, 69
networking APIs, 29
<NormalText> component, 174
npm package manager, 113, 151

O

Objective-C native modules, 116-121
onSubmitEditing prop, 25
OpenWeatherMap API, 29
organizational components, 70

P

package.json file, 113
packages, installing, 14, 113, 151
PanResponder class, 48-54
persistent data, storing, 103, 189, 203-206
Platform API, 137
platform-specific code, 133-137
position property, 84
positioning, absolute, 84-85 (see also layouts)
post release application support, 217
project structure, flashcard application, 166
Promises

Promise-based syntax, 29
working with, 213-214

R

RCTBridgeModule
    creating React Native modules, 118
    implementing, 117
    importing, 117
RCTLogInfo, 118
RCTVideo, 121
RCTVideoManager, 122
RCT_EXPORT_METHOD macro, 118
RCT_EXPORT_MODULE() macro, 118
React Native
    advantages of, 2-4
    basics of, 1
    creating components in, 8-11
    debugging packager issues, 153
    debugging tools, 145-150
    developer tools, 144
    documentation, 16
    drawbacks and risks of, 4
    JSX syntax used in, 9
    platforms supported, 1, 7, 11
    prerequisites to learning, ix
    project structure, 19-22
    rendering lifecycle, 7
    resources, xii, 160
    traditional installation, 16-22
React Navigation library, 181-187
react-native command
    creating applications using, 16
    installing developer tools, 16
    running apps on Android, 18
    running apps on iOS, 17
react-native link, 115
react-native-video component
    for Android, 127-130
    for iOS, 121-124
    installing, 115
    using, 116
react-native-web, 40
react-test-renderer package, 157
ReactVideoViewManager, 129-130
Red Screen of Death, 146-150
Redux library
    benefits of for state management, 189-190
    connecting Redux, 195-199
    defining actions, 190

About the Author

Bonnie Eisenman is a software engineer at Twitter with previous experience at Codecademy, Google, and Fog Creek Software. She has spoken at several conferences on topics ranging from React to musical programming and Arduinos. In her spare time, she enjoys building electronic musical instruments, laser-cutting chocolate, and learning languages.

Colophon

The animal on the cover of *Learning React Native* is a ringtail possum (*Pseudocheirus peregrinus*), a marsupial that is native to Australia. Ringtail possums are herbivorous and live primarily in forested regions. It is named for its prehensile tail, which is often coiled at the tip.

Ringtail possums are gray-brown in color and can grow up to 35 centimeters in length. The diet of the ringtail possum consists of a variety of leaves, flowers, and fruits. They are nocturnal and live in communal nests known as dreys. As marsupials, ringtail possums carry their young in pouches until they are developed enough to survive on their own.

The ringtail possum population declined steeply in the 1950s but has recovered in recent years. However, they are still at risk of habitat loss due to deforestation.

Many of the animals on O'Reilly covers are endangered; all of them are important to the world. To learn more about how you can help, go to *animals.oreilly.com*.

The cover image is from *Shaw's Zoology*. The cover fonts are URW Typewriter and Guardian Sans. The text font is Adobe Minion Pro; the heading font is Adobe Myriad Condensed; and the code font is Dalton Maag's Ubuntu Mono.

Learn from experts.
Find the answers you need.

Sign up for a **10-day free trial** to get **unlimited access** to all of the content on Safari, including Learning Paths, interactive tutorials, and curated playlists that draw from thousands of ebooks and training videos on a wide range of topics, including data, design, DevOps, management, business—and much more.

Start your free trial at:
oreilly.com/safari

(No credit card required)